The Legacy
of The
Consciousness

ISBN: 1 86476 338 8

Copyright © Axiom Publishing, 2005.
Unit 2, Union Street, Stepney, South Australia, 5069

AXIOM
AUSTRALIA

www.axiompublishers.com.au

Printed in Malaysia

The Legacy
of The
Consciousness

Sergio Prado-Arnuero
translator Marisa Cano

This book is dedicated with so much love to my partner Carol and to our boy Déon.

It is also is dedicated with devotion to all my Family particularly to my deceased son Sergio Antonio (Chengo). He was my Hero.

Contents

"What goes on in our mind has a direct bearing on what goes on in our body.

A key feature of the mind-body connection is that a positive attitude and stress management skills, positively impact on our general health.

If we can learn to change our mind we can change our personal well-being."

Foreword

On April 25 1991, in Strathfield, a suburb of Sydney, Australia, while at the house of friends of my brother Mario, I had the pleasure of meeting a Peruvian lady named Hermila Henríquez. We both discovered we shared a great inner affinity, and a mutual affection was sparked. As for me, a 'transcendental' friendship was born that day.

As time went by, I was able to confirm the first impression I had the moment I met her, that Mila, as we all who are lucky to be her friends call her, is one of those friendly, positive, forever smiling, ever laughing human beings who has lively conversation; is wise and tolerant without being pretentious.

During the long sessions of extremely pleasant conversation we came to share some of the events of our lives. I discovered that Mila, besides being an inexhaustible source of funny anecdotes about herself and others, had the Divine gift of knowing how to listen without becoming impatient.

I told her that in my native country, my beloved Nicaragua, I was the presenter of a radio program, know as *Doctor at Home*. This program involved answering numerous phone calls and letters, offering medical advice and making comments that were of a social-political-spiritual content. I consider that the medical approach to diseases is incomplete because it ignores the social frame in which any specific illness blooms while also overlooking the many different states of consciousness resulting from ignoring disease, and *Doctor at Home* reflected my beliefs.

'Here,' I explained to Mila, 'I feel a lesser person, living in a lovely country where I do not command the spoken language. Where my qualifications are not acknowledged and where I can't express my thoughts over the radio because of my lack of English.' I had only been in Austral for one year at that time.

'But there are programs in Spanish,' she answered. She promised to get me phone numbers, addresses and names of people I could contact and offer a program similar to the one I had been presenting in Nicoragua. Then she added, 'Okay Sergito (she often used the diminutive) imagine you've been given forty-five minutes on air, at a radio station broadcasting in Spanish. Give your program a name, write it down, along with exactly what you would like the format of the program to be, and read it to me.' The name I came up with was, *Let's Talk about Health*, I then wrote an introduction to the topic of health and disease. When I had finished, I read it to her. Perhaps because she is a very special person who always encourages others, or because she really liked it, Mila displayed great enthusiasm saying, 'Go ahead, people are going to love your program!'

Shortly afterwards I spoke to the director of Radio Australia who gave me a time slot. I then called my dear friend Rubén Fernández, of SBS who very kindly welcomed my talkback program on health which aired every Saturday.

Suddenly, I found myself writing about the subject, conducting research, talking and thinking about it day and night. Several months later I told Mila, 'I need to write a book on the topic of health and disease, but I don't know how to begin or what the title should be.'

'Do it Sergito!' she replied. 'You've got all the basics inside your head and as soon as you set pen to paper you'll do it fine!' That is how I began to write this book. Thank you, Mila!

Unfortunately, because this sort of approach is still new, I could not include every disease I would have liked.

This is a book that expresses the importance of love and the law of grace in overcoming disease. It is not always a nice book, since it urges us to take total responsibility for our state of health, something we have invested millennia trying to avoid. Its content divests us of the excuses and disguises behind which we take refuge, thus snatching from us a powerful tool for manipulation and attention-getting.

This is not a scientific book, as it diverts from the conventional scientific method, although you will find in it much scientific information, genuine and verifiable in any text of physiology, pathology or pharmacology. Likewise, it is not a religious book, as it is not framed by specific beliefs or dogma of any particular religious denomination. However, there is great religious sense in its contents and yes, spirituality is given a prevailing role.

On the other hand, it is not a fictional book, since the hypothesis it raises, in the point of view of the author, will be confirmed in the coming years. I am not implying I have already transcended all the negative situations presented, or that my life is living proof of the 'truths' contained herein. I am merely expressing my own opinion and findings.

At the same time, I am trying to lift one edge of the veil covering that marvellous and intimate communion between Body, Mind and Soul. To show there exists communion between the outer level of human beings, the waking consciousness, human beings and their own deeper levels—the Divine Breath, our Self, our Inner Shaman placed there by the Creative Force of the universe, our 'Heavenly Father', 'The Life', 'God' or whatever term you find appropriate.

Since it is a book of opinion—my opinion, the concepts and ideas in it may be shared or rejected either partially or totally by the reader. My only wish is that the reader will find this book interesting and what it says doesn't generate any negative feelings, for this is a book of love.

For this reason I dedicate this book with all my love and devotion to those entire dear to me: to the life partner Carol and our little son Déon; to my deceased biological parents Hermógenes Prado and Dolores Arnuero who were wonderful examples of responsible parenting, who showered me with their love; to all my children, especially Sergio (Chengo) who died recently and who only got to read the introduction and beginning chapters; To Mila my dear friend; to my siblings, congenial and loyal companions of my life's adventures; to Flor de Maria Lazo, a lovely old lady with hair as white as ermine's fur, who has been my mother here in Australia; and to all the Nicaraguan people.

Also to Marisa Cano my everlasting gratitude for her valuable and selfless help, and to the Latin American and Hispanic group *Aspiraciones Literarias* from Cabramatta; my love to you all.

Finally, I would like to express my deepest appreciation to my dear friend Antonio D'Laurentis without whose collaboration this book would never have been written.

LOVE AND FAITH,
THE BEST MEDICATION

'But seek ye first the kingdom of God and his righteousness, and all these things shall be added unto you.'

St Matthew 6:33

About two thousands years ago, a wonderful human being walked the land of Palestine, spreading messages of faith, hope, integrity, honesty, simplicity, humility, tolerance and forgiveness. He worked miraculous healings without the intervention of tablets, syrups, injections, chemotherapy, radiations, or long rehabilitation sessions. This was the man called Jesus.

Josephus, the Romanised Jewish historian, tells us that, more or less at about the same time Apolonius of Triana also travelled throughout Asia Minor working innumerable healings. These too were miraculous.

Since the most ancient times, when disease came to be considered the external and visible manifestation of invisible forces, the act of healing has been invested with magical religious connotations.

Civilisations that preceded us were stage and witness to doctors who simultaneously exercised the art of healing, conferring with the gods, religious rituals and the study of heavenly bodies. They were the recipients and guardians of a metaphysical esoteric knowledge based on a way of thinking that was both, at once, vertical and lineal.

The cross is a symbol of this sort of thinking in which the lineal (horizontal) thinking is united to the vertical. Probably it is the reason why Jesus symbolically, or historically, was killed on a cross. In western civilisation he is the representative of metaphysical thinking.

Truths known and utilised throughout millennia by the Lemurians, Atlanteans, Sumerians, Egyptians, Babylonians, Mesopotamians, Vedas, Hebrews, Greeks, Romans, Chinese philosophers (Lao Tzé, Confucius and Mencius), Buddhist priests, Tibetan lamas, Arabic philosophers (Sufis), Shamans of Africa and America have been hidden away and kept by a multiplicity of small groups and fraternities (secret lodges), or else they have been lovingly preserved and cultivated by the more reliable minds of aesthetics and metaphysicians who were never fond of lodges and their hierarchical systems. Lodges which are fed by the ego limiting the learning potential or the teachings of multidimensional spirits.

In the middle of the twentieth century of the Christian era, an explosive wave of metaphysical knowledge came into being once more (the Pendula movement). Those truths, known since pre-history, are re-emerging, shaking off the dust of past times, wrapped and disguised in a new terminology. Every human civilisation when extracting something from the coffers of ancient history, driven by a particularly egotistic arrogance, anoints it a new name the moment it is dusted off and put back into circulation. This promotes the idea that it has discovered something new, something never before known.

In waves similar to the flux and reflux of ocean tides, humanity approaches and distances itself from spiritual knowledge, rides on materialistic and pseudo-scientist doctrines, only to approach it again some centuries later on a different plane.

Since time immemorial, doctor-priests knew that the human being was a bio-psycho-spiritual unit. A being made in the image of the Divine Trinity, the concept of which, under one name or another, is present in almost every religion. In some books we read that the human being has a physical body, an emotional body and a mental body; others prefer to talk about a physical body, astral body and causal body; or a physical body, astral body and spirit. The ancient Egyptians talked about a physical body, its ethereal double (Ka) and the spirit (Ba).

Leaving aside the slight confusion semantic differences may cause, what is clear is that we are talking about three identities coexisting and integrated in each human being. They are filling the same corporal space and intimately merged. What we find is a physical body made up of organic matter, marvellously organised and structured, following a pattern or model that reflects a pre-existent structure of ideas and information. This pre-existent set of ideas and information is called the individual conscience, or the soul, its primary material manifestation is the DNA This identity in turn progresses, develops and perfects itself following a route suggested or traced by another inseparable companion, the one connecting it to that cosmic and superior intelligence possessing Will, who many refer to as God. This incorruptible companion we call Spirit, is the 'Divine Breath' which is forever with us.

Matter in order to acquire a pre-established form, to organise itself, to function and to come to life needs information. If we suppress this information it disintegrates, goes into putrefaction and becomes atomised. Ultimately it becomes ionised and is left to wait a new charge of information that will again process and organise it.

Information precedes organisation and resides within the conscience or soul. Some materialistic thinkers would have us believe the information is genetic and that genes and vital information are one and the same thing. However, genes and DNA are only vehicles for this information, just as a computer disk is the vehicle carrying information that can be altered, erased or reset at will by the superior conscience of the computer's programmer. In the same way, the conscience or soul imprints information on the genes, and these in turn determine the physical features, which are a reflection of the features of the conscience.

Since we are in the habit of thinking in a lineal way, we have come to believe that physical phenomena must, perforce have physical causes; chemical phenomena must have chemical causes; socio-economical phenomena must have socio-economical causes and so on. We are blind to the fact that real phenomena prior to the visible existence already exists in the dimension of the conscience or soul. When they are ready to manifest into the material world, they do so at once, on a multitude of different planes.

Lineal thinking regards the cause of anything manifesting in the material world as that which is first visualised on a particular time sequence. This is why lineal thinkers place the cause on genetic, physical, chemical, environmental or socio-economical conditions. These factors are only important conditions...no more...they are **not** the cause! Regarding this, Einstein commented: 'Breakfast is taken before lunch, but breakfast is not the cause of lunch.'

Because of the enormous number of amazing cures of diseases which are considered incurable, and came about without the use of medication, surgery or radiation, one feels compelled to wonder, 'how did such dramatic physical changes occur without the apparent intervention of physical forces?' It may be that when conventional medicine is not capable of giving hope, when all seems lost, some people excavate deeper into the coffers of their spiritual resources, pushing aside the old barriers of their fearful beliefs based on the scientific model, and to deposit their trust in a force that is beyond any measure. As a consequence they expand their own limits and deposit therapeutic hope in love and faith.

The scholars of materialism believe that faith is antagonistic to reason. I believe that faith is antagonistic and incompatible with fear, while at the same time being complimentary to reason. Faith is only another extremely strong universal law that when applied may generate amazing changes. As a universal law faith is a pillar of life. When Jesus of Nazareth, the Divine Teacher, commanded 'get up and walk' he had no need to rely on his own faith, for he lived in communion with the 'Father' and in the knowledge of the laws of life. Jesus did not use his faith, because he had the knowledge that when he said, 'your faith has healed you' he was using the faith of the person being healed.

The faith we need to heal always depends on the personality of each of us. The Bible says: 'He, to whom much has been given, much will be asked from him'. The breach between faith and reason is what leads to deviation. When we separate faith from reason we distance ourselves from both.

The scientific medical struggle against cancer is the product of a false attachment to reason devoid of faith. This struggle leads to a chain of frustrations and failures, meanwhile the number of cases that have been cured following an alternative therapeutic method accumulates. The Inquisition of ancient times, as with terrorism of today are products of a false faith devoid of reason and compassion. It is still leading to the most abject crimes and unspeakable atrocities performed supposedly in the name of faith. Only when faith, reason, love and compassion conjugate do the great works of humanity emerge.

Our conscience is in constant debate between two basic feelings, love and fear, with each capable of manifesting in many forms. For all the infinite forms in which love can be manifested, there is a corresponding opposite derived from fear. To the trilogy formed by love, faith and hope; fear responds with hatred, panic and desperation. Calmness is confronted by agitation, peace is confronted by anger and war. Assertive self-esteem is confronted by a demonstrative and power-hungry ego. A loving relationship as a manifestation of tenderness is confronted by a sexual relationship of domination and power. Humility is confronted by arrogance; understanding by intolerance, and health by illness.

Illness is not a natural state of the human being. Diseases are alterations of our conscience manifesting at different levels, at a bio-chemical level by alteration of the secretion of neuro-transmitters or by modification of the neuro-receptors. At a physical level by pain, drowsiness, fever, headache, hyper-activity etcetera. At an emotional level, by depression, anguish, anxiety, anger, impatience, hatered and resentment, all of which have negative consequences at a social level. Precisely because of this intimate relationship between mind, body and soul, diseases are capable of being cured by spiritual means. Spiritual healing exists and is genuine. A Hebrew saying assures us that 'a happy heart is a good medicine'.

Health is a state of harmony, balance, equilibrium and integration of the physical, astral and spiritual bodies within the individual, which at the same time invariably integrates the person with creation. Everything has a repercussion on everything else. We cannot vibrate harmoniously with the universe if we are not in harmony with our own being, our self, our consciousness. How can we expect to command that which surrounds us if we are not in command of our own selves?

Illness is a path full of signals and signs leading us back to integration. We live surrounded by signs that we don't interpret. Disease is not a product, a companion, a consequence of fragmentation, but fragmentation itself. Health is integration, and integrity.

Modern medicine is a separatist; fragmenting science. It has, therefore, become an anti-science, anti-knowledge, and anti-wisdom movement loaded with information, dressed up in the rags of knowledge and stripped of wisdom. It has become more dehumanised because it has lost contact with the Divinity and does not feel reverence for life any longer. It has become more and more depersonalised as a logical consequence of its fragmentary and separatist tendencies.

To prove this let us listen to a dialogue taking place every morning in a hospital ward when the Doctor arrives to check on patients: 'Anything new in the ward?'

'Well, in the bed thirty-four we have a fractured femur, the x-rays and blood test are ready. In number forty, we have a traumatised pneumothorax, in number eighteen we have a cerebrovascular accident of the right temporal lobe.' Each day, doctors know more and more about tests and examinations, analysis and diseases, and less and less about the patient. One wonders if the human being behind the disease is important any longer?

A doctor should be a good friend who helps us become ourselves by finding the path that exists within ourselves. When someone accidentally suffers the amputation of a limb and are rapidly taken to the hospital, where following a meticulous wash of both segments the amputated segment is surgically reset in its place, we say the limb was 'saved'. In fact healing must, perforce, go along the path of salvation. Salvation means reconciliation with our own nature, 're-integration'. We are *saved* when we are whole. Integrity is impossible without faithfulness, loyalty and love towards ourselves.

Regarding this, my favourite poet, the Mexican Amado Nervo, writes as follows. Unfortunately, although the poem is a good translation into English it has lost the rhythm and musicality that was present in its Spanish form:

Search within yourself
For the solution to all your problems,
Even those you may consider
Most external and material.
Even when crossing the virgin jungle,
Even when building a bridge,
Even when raising a wall,
You must first search
For the secret within yourself.

Within yourself;
Already the bridges are built
And all the structures raised within yourself.
Ask the invisible Architect!
He will give you his formulae
And provide you with the most efficient of tools,
And you will always succeed.
For within yourself lies the key
To all the secrets.

Human beings, individually and collectively, tend to place outside of themselves the responsibility for all their suffering, including disease. In their eagerness to justify this outward projection, and as a corollary to a previous fragmentation, because we fail to see polar unity existing in everything, we also fragment disease. We talk about health in the singular, not about healths, since health is a singular state of harmony, balance and integrity...in a word, *well-being*.

Similarly, there are no diseases, but a singular state of disharmony, imbalance, lack of integrity...in one word, *illness*. The scientific method; where the same group of symptoms are reproduced in the presence of the same supposed 'causal' agent, and which apparently justifies the belief in the existence of multiple and different diseases, is incomplete because it cannot explain the occurrence of healthy carriers. Some people are carriers of viruses and germs deemed by science as being the 'cause' of disease. They enjoy a state of well-being themselves, even though they may have been carrying these micro organisms for many years.

Pragmatic and scientific materialism likes to justify these cases arguing the great efficiency of these individual's immune system. These scientists are unaware that this efficient immune system is but one of the many manifestations of harmony, balance, integrity and well-being of these individuals as a whole.

I would regret it if the reader interprets harmony, balance and integrity as a reflection of morality, I am not moralising. The moral frame is closely related with cultural perceptions and is constantly changing. I am talking about the individual's perception system that enables people to maintain a reasonable peace of mind regardless of external changes around themselves.

At this point in time after centuries of fighting against disease and taking into account the achievements publicised by the Medical Guild regarding the eradication of infectious diseases, there should not be any ill people at all. Human beings should be healthy and almost immortal. Nevertheless the correlation between the healthy and the ill is still practically the same as in past centuries. All we have really achieved is to shift symptoms and syndromes we had incorrectly named 'diseases'.

In this way, we eliminated gonorrhea, but we are scourged by syphilis; we eliminated syphilis and AIDS appears. The number of deaths due to infection is decreasing, but deaths due to traffic accidents are on the increase. In any given society, we eliminate malnutrition and rickets, but obesity, diabetes, heart attacks, cerebra-vascular accidents and cholesterol problem increase. Also the demand for psychiatrists, psychologists and counsellors increases in response to the growing incidence of juvenile delinquency, alcoholism, drug addiction and so on. The ratio remains intact, because we are still searching 'without' for what lies 'within'.

The visible and external manifestations of the different states of conscience are considered 'causes' and treated as such. In suppressing this type of communication, we are forcing the conscience to shift to other areas in order to make us aware of its message waiting to be redeemed. In as far as the individual's conscience changes and evolves, so too do the features and characteristics of the physical body that serves as its means of expression. The areas of imbalance are shifted to other levels of the conscience and, consequently, there is a change in the type of 'disease' suffered in this new state. This explains why there is child, juvenile, adult and old age disease, some typical of the third world and others of the developed and industrialised world.

I have intentionally avoided talking about diseases 'pertaining' to any stage in life. In this case I don't like the term, nor do I consider it appropriate, since it conveys a message of 'belonging to' and 'inherent to'. The truth is that neither do we belong to the disease, nor does the disease belong to us. A disease is only a path that leads us to knowledge, acceptance and re-encountering our Divine roots, 'Life' itself, our internal shaman. It can also lead us to depression, desperation and total separation from our origins, through an egotistic aggravation of the condition acting as a dense fog which causes us to lose sight of this path. Could this be behind suicide or euthanasia?

Our conscience is constantly calling for harmony and balance between the physical, social, astral and spiritual planes. The search for learning and re-establishment of this harmony can happen in a voluntary, conscious and enjoyable way, through knowledge, or in a natural and almost unconscious way through simple and loving faith. It is not achieved through religious fanaticism, which has never been an offspring of love, but is rather an extension of the hatred and arrogance of the ego.

When we refuse to reach this balance, a disease seeking to show us the path to re-establish the balance, overcomes us. If we eliminate the disease with pharmaceutical weapons and without listening to the message of our conscience the true causal agent, our conscience will manifest itself on other planes in order to send the message again. Thus, a shift in symptoms is all we would have achieved.

To accept that the responsibility of our state of health or illness lies within us is a difficult step to take. People would rather visit a medical practitioner, ask for a specific diagnosis (we love to give a name to our illness), and come out with two or three pharmaceutical medications to take or inject. They prefer this to the inconvenience of a conscientious self-examination in finding out what message the disease is sending and then making the necessary changes in order to restore their own balance.

It is easier and more comfortable to believe that a virus floating in the atmosphere causes the problem affecting our airways, rather than to invest time and honesty in analysing fears and phobias. Since this means we will later have to work at making the necessary changes to our frame of mind and perception system in order to eliminate this fear, and with it the problem with our airways. It is easier to think in terms of allergy as a phenomenon independent of our thoughts and attitudes in order not to face the fact that this 'allergy' is the visible manifestation at a physical level of intolerance at a mental and emotional level.

27

Allergy is a consequence of intolerance, and we would do better examining our attitudes towards the opposite sex, other races, nationalities, cultures, families, social classes, generations and other ways of thinking. We should, likewise, look at our attitude toward animals and climatic changes over which we have no control. Intolerance reflects lack of acceptance, and lack of acceptance is not the offspring of love, but of the ego.

Once we learn to say 'let it be so' not in a mechanical way, but consciously and genuinely, then we begin to grow. An adequate contact with the Divinity requires acceptance. We must learn to say: 'Speak my Lord, your servant listens,' or 'Thy Will be done.'

THE SHAMAN WITHIN

'The God who dwells within my breast can deeply stir my inmost being. He who is enthroned on high above my strength cannot move a thing outside myself.'

Goethe, *Faust*

An extreme degree of lack of acceptance is the thirst for control, domination and power. People love power because they believe power will afford them the opportunity to buy or acquire goods, fortune, fame, sexual pleasure, obedience and control over others. This anxious and desperate search for power is not the offspring of love or of a healthy and well-founded self-esteem, it is the child of an arrogant and demonstrative ego.

We consider the disease on its own as a live, albeit defective entity, that forces the patient to invest a great deal of energy and attention to it. Then for the same reason, it also offers others the opportunity to focus their attention on the sufferer. Love and hate are both attention-grabbing phenomena. We place a lot of loving protection, understanding and tender attention on the objects of our love. Ego is born out of the fear of not being able to inspire and receive this kind of attention. No one can give that which they lack. Therefore, those who have an abundance of love will offer love, while those who have abundance of fear, impose fear.

Since the ego or 'secondary I', as it is called by the Sufis (Arab philosophers), is a master of disguise and a trickster, it hides the fear it uses and moulds itself under a mask of self-sufficiency, over-confidence and arrogance. One proverb states, 'Tell me what you boast of, and I'll tell you what you lack'.

Fear, which in itself is a terrible counsellor, creates in us resentment and hatred. It locks us in a supposedly protective shell, deforms our frame of perception, wrap us up in a cloud of negative thinking and can isolate us from others. In other instances it transforms us into bitter, hostile and domineering beings. In others, who refuse to hate, as it becomes more acute it can provoke a disorder known as 'panic disorder'.

Shyness born from the fear of social contact, rejection or the feeling of inadequacy, must not to be confused with the aloofness of some human beings who, not fearing social contact, love their solitude because it offers them the opportunity to be alone with their greater friend; the internal shaman, their inner self. Dialogue with this great friend, the 'Primary I', and the contact with the Divinity through prayer, meditation or introspection, is a comfort painful to renounce once we've learnt to enjoy it. Regarding this I have included the following quotations:

> *'If you know how to be on your own, you'll be your own master'.*
> —Leonardo Da Vinci

> *'Solitude is the privilege of all extraordinary men'.*
> —Shoppenhauer

'To my solitude I go, from my solitude I come, to walk along with myself my own thoughts are enough'.
—Lope de Vega

'The solitary man is a beast...or a God!'.
—Aristotle

The thirst for control, domination and obedience is the seed of frequent frustration. Frustration is a negative emotion going hand in hand with thoughts that share their 'affinity of resonance'. Both stimulate the suprarenal glands to secrete large doses of catecholamines, adrenaline and nor-adrenaline. Simultaneously, they stimulate the nerve cells to secrete neuro-transmitters like serotonin or dopamine. All these substances either trigger or stop a series of physical, mental, cardio-vascular, muscular and metabolic reactions known as 'the fright, fight, and flight reaction'.

People who suddenly face a fall from a certain height, or a fight, or danger become frightened and trigger a multitude of mental and physical reactions that affect all their organs and their whole being. People with negative emotions and thoughts, are loaded with catecholamines and serotonins, which keep them in a chronic state of fright, fight, flight reaction. This state calls for metabolic disorders of triglycerides and cholesterol; hemodynamic disorders like high blood pressure; local blood circulation disorders, that when present in the heart is called angina pectoris, and when present in the brain acquires the characteristics of cluster headaches or migraines.

The entire chain and sequence of physical and bio-chemical changes happening inside us are closely related to our perception system, our way of thinking and our emotions. If sustained for a long time these changes may affect our DNA and our genes. The chairman of this amazing laboratory of genetic engineering is our conscience, our own piece of life, our own breath of God, our internal shaman.

UNITY AND POLARITY

'Superhuman intelligence has, from the beginning, made use of three mediums of expression—men, animals and plants. In each of which Life pulsates in a different rhythm.'

The I Ching Richard Wilhelm

The symbolic legend about the dawn of humanity, when Adam and Eve inhabited the Garden of Eden, where diseases did not exist and where they could see and talk with the Creator and maintain a loving and friendly relationship with all the animal species, tell us about oneness.

The path of healing must, necessarily, travel along the path of 'sanctification'. Sanctification meaning, not devout beatitude but the search for 'oneness', in as far as we understand that the apparent diversity of the universe is a multitude of forms of manifestation, at infinitely different levels, of the one and only reality…the Divinity, God…Life itself. Our eyes, senses and mind will learn to observe and to love this gigantic common base and the infinite variety of similarities shared by all living creatures who make up the cells of this great cosmic organism: the Universe.

God is that universal intelligence in possession of a Will of His own. God is Life and Life itself is God. God is the Absolute…The Unity. God is represented as the number one, which is the origin of all numbers and is the only one contained in all of them (a piece of God, Life, is contained in every creature). For example, the number five contains five times the number one and the number ten contains ten times the number one. The number one is indivisible and multiplied by itself is always one. One is eternal. One is in everything and is everywhere. One is spaceless and timeless; and there are no contrasts in one.

In this way one extracts two (the Son of One) from itself, and to soften the contrast between one and two, three is born. Essentially, these numbers are the basis for all existing numbers. All steps in creation are triple steps. Life (God) uses a trinitarian model of manifestation. The same happens in Dialectics: Thesis = 1, Antithesis = 2 and synthesis = 3. In religion it is: the Father, the Son and the Holy Ghost for Christians; Osiris, Isis and Horus for the ancient Egyptians; Brahma, Vishnú and Shiva for the Brahmans. Almost every religion talks about a trinity, albeit under different names. If we move on to study the different branches of knowledge, we also find a trinity there: science, religion and philosophy, craftily separated by man, but actually parts of a 'unit' at the knowledge level.

In nuclear physics, Nobel Prize winner Murray Gell-Mann coined a word to name an unknown entity. That word is 'Quark', an atomic sub-particle with a fractional electric charge. It is divided into three parts: a 'Park', with two thirds of the charge; a 'Nark' and a 'Lark', which make up the other third of the charge. The nucleus of an atom would, therefore, be made up of this strange triple entity: the Trinitarian model of Life.

If the quark really exists then it is a triple part unit, meaning 'three in one' and 'one in three' just like the Holy Trinity of various religions and our three dimensional space or the three musketeers of Alex Dumas. This show us that unity is forever present within multiplicity, which is only a form of manifestation of this unity or oneness.

The Adam-like man in the Garden of Eden was still within oneness. He was healthy, eternal, could see the face and hear the voice of Life, the Creator. He didn't know right or wrong, since both are opposing concepts, which do not exist within the 'Oneness'. He ate the forbidden fruit of knowledge. 'You will become like Gods and you will know right and wrong!' and so he entered the world of contrasts, the world of multiple options, the world of heroism but also the world of diseases. I will not say the world of 'sin', because this is a word that has moral connotations and it pre-supposes a judgmental attitude.

In this world of opposing contrasts of vital cycles within which, one of its poles is death, love stands as a great and universal cohesive force. The return to the Garden of Eden is a return to the Divine, to unity and integrity. It is a return to the holistic. Its path is through reverence, through love for every form of life, beginning with ourselves.

It is impossible for the human being, because of their conditioning, to see unity in a world of physical phenomena. We see and judge the opposite sides of physical phenomenon as separate, opposite, antagonistic phenomena, one excluding the other. It is hard, if not impossible for us, to see both poles simultaneously and to understand that they are complementary and parts of the same oneness and that the existence of one depends on the other.

We think in terms of black or white, light or shadow, hot or cold, good or evil, right or left and masculine or feminine as separate and opposite realities. Hot and cold are only extremes of the same element—temperature. Clarity and shadow are both the product of light, because objects can only project a shadow if there is light. If we were to eliminate light we would have darkness, not shadows.

In the same way, right and left are relative positions. In a mirror, the movement of your right hand corresponds to the same movement of your left hand. Black and white are connected through a continuity of colours and tonalities. One is the sum of all colours, while the other is the absence of colour; therefore, both are simply two poles of the same path.

The poles of any given reality do not exclude each other, but depend on one another for their existence. The movement between one pole and its opposite is called a cycle, and life in all its forms is made up of cycles. To be healthy is to be balanced, to harmoniously synthetize our vital cyclical movements with the vital cyclical movements of the universe. To be healthy is to know how to be in harmony with the immanent movement of things, it is to leave behind our polar prejudices in order to be able to see and love the unity in everything around us.

This movement or cycle between two extremes is clearly understood in our respiratory and circulatory systems. We cannot breathe out unless previously we breathed in. Our heart will not have a systole (contraction) unless it also has a diastole (expansion). For the sea to have a high tide it needs a low tide. Only when the moon reaches its last quarter can it start on its way to full moon again.

It is in this way that we must understand and accept that our body is ruled by the same rhythmical laws of these cyclic movements. To love each and every one of these cyclic movements is to love our own reality. One should not violate it or spend their life fighting it. Those who live in peace and harmony with their own reality have self-esteem, and those who enjoy self-esteem are on their way to overcome and transcend their ego. Those who transcend ego transcend fear; those who live without fear, live in love; those who have love have God; those who have God enjoy health.

The opposite of oneness and unitarian tendencies is separatism. It is the root of all prejudice, discrimination and man-made borders which divide humanity e.g. nationalism, racism, classism, elitism, machoism, feminism, capitalism, communism, scientism, materialism, Catholicism, Christianity, Islamism and so on.

The acceptance of our own cycles, including the cycles of everything around us, and being in harmony with the world while holding loving, Unitarian thoughts, are the tools that will open the doors to the lost paradise. There we will live in health, invulnerable to disease and aging, as well as being in direct and conscious contact with the Divinity, which manifests itself in the mineral, vegetable, animal and human kingdoms.

The structure of society has been built thinking not of our physical or emotional health, not of an eternal frame of ethics, but of productivity. All fields of human activity working toward that 'good' science doesn't escape this general trend. Science is not, never has been and never will be neutral and without a hidden agenda and medicine is not an exception. The medical model of diseases is a weapon of capitalism and of the domineering cultures, races and social class. It was a model extremely useful to Adolf Hitler and his theory of race supremacy. It opens the doors to genetic manipulation with all the ethical implications and consequences.

To choose the road where we are attempting to modify the genetic or the bio-chemical map in order to achieve permanent improvement of the human race, instead of attempting to modify our attitudes in order to achieve the same; is to choose the way of the quick fix and in every field of human activity this way has proven to be a failure.

At the end of this road there is only two winners: the pharmacological corporations and the medical organisations that work in close association with them.

Medicine is no longer a priesthood, no longer a communion between the doctor and the patient. Medicine is only another branch of industry, a booming business. Thinking about this in 1996 I felt inclined to write a poem to express this feeling.

Sabotaging the Foundations of Prejudice

People's beliefs must be shaken,
Sabotaging the foundations of prejudice.
And the dams of the mind must be emptied,
Turning our sacrifice into disagreement.

Let us understand that the secret of 'The Eternal'
Is not to be found in syrups or injections,
Pills or in modern pharmaceuticals,
Or in the different radiation rooms.

For a doctor cannot, unwittingly,
Recur to the great pharmacopoeia
In order to restore health in patients
Who have distanced themselves from love, the
     Panacea.

Where does the struggle and anxiety,
That humans fabricate in their insistence
To adjust themselves to society, take them,
But to frustration and agony.

When in our final footsteps,
As we prepare our departure for the tomb,
Do we discover there is an absence of social
Differences in the afterlife?

It is then that we come face to face
With the drama of a life that has passed by,
It is then that our mind becomes crowded
With the memories of deceased love.

It is then that we feel the emptiness
That ambition has sowed in our Soul,
And we even discover the meaning of a life
Lived in healthy communion.

Of a life lived in harmony with the times,
With the valleys, the rivers and mountains,
With our neighbour, with our feelings
And even with those maligned pests!

It is not a matter of fighting against fate
And of holding on to life and its ties,
It is not a matter of letting cretins
Insert needles in our bodies and limbs.

Just allow those mysterious hands,
That lead to a life beyond
In another, more loving dimension,
Slide over your body.

Become the priest of your inner temple,
Binding together heaven and the abyss,
Learn to transcend yourself through your Soul
A traveller of times gone by.

And maybe...oh, the twist of life!
That which seemed so meaningless,
Once your fighting has lost its obstinacy,
Will recover what was deemed forever lost.

WHEN DO WE BEGIN TO LEARN
...IN PAST LIVES?

'For all the prophets and the law prophesized until John. And if ye will receive it, this is Elijah, who was to come.
He that hath ears to hear, let him hear.'
St Matthew 11:13,-15

'And his disciples asked him, saying, why then say the scribes that Elijah must first come?
And Jesus answered and said unto them: Elijah truly shall first come and restore all things.
But I say onto you that Elijah is come already and they knew him not, but have done unto him whatsoever they listed. Likewise shall also the Son of Man suffer of them.
Then disciples understood that he spake unto them of John the Baptist.'
St Matthew 17:10.-13

When do we begin to learn? This is a hard question to answer with precision. In the archives of knowledge within every human being are many episodes recorded along with an infinite quantity of information, not belonging to their own, exclusive, personal experience, at least not from their present lives. Every human being has in store a millenary, probably even pre-historic wisdom, apparently hidden away in the sub-conscious, or in the astral body, or in the depths of the spirit. In any case, beyond the reach of the senses; in the supra-conscious of our innermost being. Unaware of it, we keep in store an immeasurable amount of life experiences other than those from our present life. These we call family memories, racial memories and knowledge that can be embodied in what Carl Jung and other metaphysicians call, 'The Great Collective Unconscious'.

This great collective unconscious, might store all the vital experiences of our species and of all other animal species which inhabit the planet, along with all the vital experiences of the mineral and vegetable kingdoms. This collective unconscious is what we call 'instinct' when it saves us from a danger we could not otherwise have foreseen in any rational way. In reality, it is a knowledge so perfect, profound and great that it impregnates and inundates each and every one of our body and brain cells, surfacing at such speed that it is impossible for us to be aware of it at a conscious level.

Even before birth, human beings are already aware of danger. The spermatozoon instinctively knows which way to move in it's eagerness to prolong its existence. Live beings flee from danger; search for food; avoid that which causes them pain or suffering and crave for copulation in order to obtain pleasure and reproduce — this we call 'survival instinct'. Even before being taught, human beings already have a natural notion of good and evil—this is the conscience! I ask those who like to talk about instinct the following: 'Is this then a moral instinct?'

From the very first records of history, including the Stone Age paintings, we know that in every civilisation and era, in every continent and race, human beings have held a firm belief in Divinity. A religious instinct?

In that case, what is really learnt? How much of what we learn now, is acquired for the first time? Could it be that we are just awakening, at a conscious level, knowledge that had been lying dormant in the subconscious for maybe millions of years?

According to many metaphysicians, to learn and to awaken are part of the same process. Knowledge, family and racial memories of our species and other species, engraved in the subconscious of our minds, is also engraved in the subconscious of our reproductive cells (ovules and spermatozoon) through the DNA in our genes. 'As it is above, so it is below', 'as in the macro-cosmos, so it is in the micro-cosmos', this is the law of correspondence formulated thirty or more centuries ago by Hermes Trimegisto. Transforming these instinctive and subconscious memories and knowledge into conscious memories and knowledge is what we call 'learning'. Is learning then simply a process of remembering?

Because of a special biological behaviour, which in the long run turns acquired traits into hereditary, following generations will progressively be more 'awake and conscious' if we ourselves awaken and raise all those useful instincts to a conscious level. By contrast if we insist on awakening our most aggressive instincts— those that proved useful for our survival and reproduction in times when totally different biological and social conditions existed on the planet—following generations will experience an authentic biological and spiritual regression.

Learning to learn is learning to awaken, to remember and to re-establish our contact with the Divinity; with Oneness. Perhaps that is why aesthetics and philosophers are forever searching for solitude— different from loneliness which carries with it a connotation of misfortune, grief, something not looked for, and something fatal! On the other hand, solitude is a very searched for, and desirable, state of isolation, which far from bringing us suffering offers us the opportunity for prayer, meditation and exploratory introspection, leading us to re-encounter our divine roots and that immensely wise 'Collective Unconscious'.

In conventional medical texts, learning problems are often linked to Attention Deficits, Autism, Asperger Syndrome etcetera. Let go back to the law of correspondence: 'as it is above, so it is below'; As it is within, so it is without; As it is in the macro, so it is in the micro. He who cannot fix his attention on the inside, finds it difficult to fix it on the outside. He who cannot dream and love his dreams, cannot wake up and learn happily. As this society does not know how to love dreams that go far away from the society's dream and goals, it tends to label, and brand as carriers of disorder, any one who walks a different way in learning. If we are not allowed to perceive the present in love, we will find it difficult to recall the past and love the future.

As far as society and the media become more and more identified with pragmatic, materialistic and competitive ideals, human beings will move further away from an authentic spirituality. They will lose their way in their search for oneness and become confused about their integration process and when this happens they fragment and consequently become ill.

Disease as such, by itself, whatever the form it takes—diabetes, arthritis, high blood pressure, asthma, cancer, multiple sclerosis, psoriasis etcetera—is pointing at only one learning problem. Disease is the vehicle for a message of redemption. Healing comes when we learn to love our dreams, our roots, race, language, parents, offspring, reality, present, past, future, experiences, mistakes, gender, differences, similarities, environment and everything around us. Healing comes when we start feeling a genuine reverence for life.

We heal when we stop saying: 'If I only had what I used to have,' or when we stop believing that the time for happiness will come once we have that which we do not yet have. He who knows how to love and enjoy his dreams, will wake up to happiness, for each dream will recall something beautiful—or at least interesting—of what is kept in that information bank called the Cosmic Intelligence, the Divinity or just simply Life.

For practical purposes in this, our present life, we may start from the premise that the learning process begins inside the womb. Psychiatrists, spiritualists and metaphysicians (myself included) are more aware each day that the learning process was initiated for each and everyone of us from the earliest manifestation of life somewhere in the universe.

For those who believe that God is one and everywhere without fragmenting, God is All and All is unitarian, All is oneness. Within this oneness languages and idioms are not important any more, since each of them has been inspired and born from the mind of the All, and the All understands everything.

Man lived within this oneness in the Garden of Eden. As the Bible states, Adam could look at the face of God and speak directly with Him. He did not know good or evil. Good and evil are opposite concepts born from polarity, from the world of contrasts, from multiplicity not from the oneness, since oneness has no contrast. Adam was not in a world of polarity, but within oneness. However, he ate from the forbidden fruit taken from the tree of knowledge and suddenly found himself in a world of polarity, he became aware of his nakedness, the difference between good and evil, hot and cold, night and day, prey and predator, men and women, black and white and so on. None of these differences existed in the Garden of Eden before he ate from the tree of knowledge—the tree of contrasts.

The human being is still within this oneness inside its mother's womb. The merging between the Yin and the Yang, the masculine and the feminine elements, the spermatozoon and the ovule took place not long ago. The embryo is still one with the earthly being who gave it life; its mother. While in the womb, it does not interpret literally every word spoken by people around it, as it can perceive the ideas and feelings they carry. It can feel if it is wanted or rejected, if the mother or father are making plans to terminate its life or if they are lovingly awaiting its birth.

The embryo can feel the emotional charge of its surroundings, and no matter what language is spoken, it understands because it is still within the oneness. It can perceive the message of music in any language (even the hidden message when reversing the tape...see footnote at the end of this chapter). In its first attempts to understand or foresee the waiting polarity it will be guided and influenced by the adults around it. Inside the mother's womb it can receive musical, mathematical or language tuition. Its racial or species memories can be refreshed before birth in order to ease its future learning process.

If the mother takes drugs there is, inside her womb, a wonderful being in unity with her who quickly learns to be dependent on, and thereby become addicted to, those drugs. Within the women's body grows a marvellous seed, full of beauty and potential harmony. A compendium of tenderness, joy, healthy vitality, intelligence and great evolutionary potential. But beware, this embryo can retrograde as well! To a certain degree, it depends on its parents for the direction in which its first steps will head. There inside that humid and warm womb resides a human being connected mainly with its mother, with its mother's thoughts and feelings, with what his/her mother eats, drinks, swallows, inhales or injects.

The child's main seat of learning is its mother and upon her it mainly depends on awakening those dormant experiences that will stimulate its development into a spiritually solid, humanly tender and protective person or into a bitter, dependent, resentful being loaded with hatred and anger.

Within all of us, lies the wisdom of every race and civilisation. There is nothing new under the sun or beyond it. What is new, is that which for billions of years has remained hidden waiting to be uncovered, or lain dormant waiting to be awakened.

Perhaps because within us, our primary I, immensely wise and connected to the cosmic information bank, knows all. Amado Nervo, the great Mexican poet, left us this wonderful thought:

> Search within yourself
> For the solution to all your problems,
> Even those you may consider
> More external and material.
> Even when crossing the virgin jungle,
> Even when throwing a bridge,
> Even when raising a wall,
> You must first search
> For the secret within yourself.
>
> Within yourself;
> Already the bridges are thrown.
> And all the structures are raised within yourself.
> Ask to the invisible architect!
> He will give you his formulae
> And provide you with the most efficient of tools,
> And you will always succeed.
> For within you lies the key
> To all the secrets.

This mysterious key to all secrets is the Divine Breath that Life placed in every one of us. The Sufi philosophers call it The Primary I, as opposed to the secondary I, which western psychiatrists and psychologists call the Ego.

Footnote: When we record music on a tape, simultaneously and without being aware, we are recording some hidden words that can be heard when reversing the tape. It is not easy to hear, but there currently exist some specific equipment that analyses the voice, so that we can hear when reversing the tape. This voice is the subconscious voice. There is developing a branch of psychology based on what is called reverse speech.

THE COLLECTIVE UNCONSCIOUS

'However men may differ in disposition and in education, the foundation of human nature is the same in everyone. And every human being can draw in the course of his education from the inexhaustible wellspring of the Divine in man's nature. But here likewise two dangers threaten: a man may fail in his education to penetrate to the real roots of humanity and remain fixed in convention—a partial education of this sort is as bad as none—or he may suddenly collapse and neglect his self development.'

Richard Wilhelm *The I Ching*

Eternal and immeasurable wisdom, that doesn't know space nor time nor limiting borders was known, respected and worshipped from the most remote ancient times. The zealous materialistic scientists that proclaimed and popularised the so-called 'Scientific Method' led western civilisation to christen this loving, wise and cohesive force of the universe as the Collective Unconscious. This is a cold term and although it satisfactorily explains a great number of mental and emotional processes, it does not stimulate the loving search for oneness, the only path for us to achieve unique harmony with the cosmos.

The term Collective Unconscious is useful when explaining inexplicable phenomena without plunging into religious controversy. It also gives a certain air of intellectuality to the person using it, but it distracts us from the concept of Divinity. It is not a matter of trying to prove it is false, since it is not. It is, rather, to prove that the Collective Unconscious, although it truthfully and logically explains a good deal of mental and emotional manifestations, is not their cause. The Collective Unconscious is no more than a specific level of manifestation of a superior, eternal and greater reality—Life itself—that which some call God.

The acceptance of a Collective Unconscious pre-supposes the existence of a Collective Mind. Could this Collective Mind be the sum of all the active minds that have existed since the beginning of life in the universe? If so, are the minds from remote times present today as a result of the transmission of racial and species memories through genetically transmissible messages in the DNA (Desoxyribonucleic Acid) of chromosomes and genes? Or, is there an evolutionary kind of conscience which, through infinite life cycles (reincarnations), evolves towards perfection while retaining deep-layer memories from remote times?

Geneticists assume that messages hidden in our genes are primarily responsible for our personality, behaviour, physical looks, the effectiveness of our immune system, longevity, diseases, preferences and so on. Astrologers believe that the cause of all of this lies not in the genetic map, but in the Astral map of the individual at the moment of their birth. They say, our personal characteristics depend on the position of the stars and satellites of our solar system: the year, month, day and exact hour of our birth in relation to the place where it happened.

Sociologist believe the structure and functioning of the societies in which we are born and live influence and mould our body, mind, behaviour, attitudes and customs. There are thousands of conscious acts which seem to prove, almost beyond doubt, the truth of the suppositions, discoveries and conclusions of geneticists, astrologers and sociologists. Many people believe that the degree of evolution, our characteristics and the infinite variety of affinities of resonance a particular conscience has, before it is incarnated, determines and causes the astral and genetic maps that represent it precisely and adequately at those levels.

Our physical, mental and emotional traits are no more than representations of the same conscience at a physical, mental and emotional level, since all these planes are simultaneously representing the one and only superior reality—the conscience. They coincide perfectly, and this is what makes astrologers and geneticists of lineal thinking believe that the astral or genetic maps are the cause of physical, mental and emotional make-up.

Before incarnating, the conscience must choose (or have chosen for it) a race, a country, a language, a family and a particular society that can match it, therefore, can represent it as well. All of this happens in order to help the individual conscience continue its evolutionary learning within the framework of its own affinities of resonance.

Thus, when the resonance of the social or collective conscience of a country changes abruptly, as occurs in revolutions, many souls flee in search of other social groups that have a resonance more in keeping with their own. Violent economical or warlike movements have triggered most of the massive migrations of human beings. Wars are one of the last external manifestations in a long chain resulting from particular states of consciousness.

When a particular conscience discovers that its possibilities for development and evolution cannot be achieved within the society it was born, it transmits its urge to travel to other countries. Other countries where there are societies with different structures that will help change its perception system to the mind and body in which it incarnated.

It is the accepted case among medical and psychiatric circles, that the existence of an unconscious and collective mind lives in active interconnection with the personal unconscious and conscious mind. If we accept that emotional disturbances can become somatic, organic and manifest at a physical level–as proved by the ever-growing list of psychosomatic diseases, then why is it so difficult for us to accept that any chemical, physical, historical, electrical and social manifestations in the planet is only that...a manifestation!

Simultaneous manifestations of a superior and invisible reality at an infinite variety of levels. This immense, omnipresent, omnipotent, harmonious and loving superior reality, invisible and apparently undetectable to our body senses is life itself. The Chi of the Taoists, The Great Spirit of Native Americas or what some others call God.

Life, or God, is the primary cause of everything manifesting at infinite variety of levels. The expulsion from the Garden of Eden is a symbolism reflecting the estrangement of the human race from its Divine roots. Life and Life's reverence is the path to healing any disease, be it a personal, family, social, mental, emotional, environmental or physical disease. Healing is a journey in which we are returning to oneness; to our Divine roots, to loving and respecting life in all its various forms.

All this has been explained only as an attempt to reveal this author's belief, which is neither original or exclusive to him. A belief that physical, mental and social processes hide to some—or reveal to others—working at a conscience level.

The future of medicine lies not in the exaggerated growth of the pharmacological arsenal, but in teaching and learning, with love, to re-establish the links with our Divine roots. It is something that we as individuals and as a species are obliged to realise.

Our roots are not limited by an artificial concept of nationality, race, religion, language or even humanness. They are immersed deeply in life itself. We are part of the eternal life, living at the moment, a human experience.

We must stop trying to dominate and control nature and try to live in harmony with it. Respect it, love it and cooperate with it.

PERSONALITY TYPE A

'Thus also the *man of calling*:
He sees the difficulties.
The Tao of Heaven does not quarrel
And yet has the gifts necessary to be victorious.
He does not speak
And yet he finds the right answer.
He does not beckon
And yet everything comes of itself.
He is tranquil
And yet he is competent in planning.
Heaven's nets are wide meshed
But they lose nothing.'

Lao Tse *The Tao Teh Ching*

There has been some neglect in studying different types of personalities. However, it appeals to my sense of irony that industrialised societies promote the adoption of a particular personality type. A personality type that is considered as the epitome of responsibility and hard-working. Then after they have fostered this personality type they then baptise it as a disorder.

This personality disorder has been significantly well studied and is called Personality Type A. A great deal has been published about this type of personality and each provides a similar description. Consequently, I won't pretend to be original in the description I am about to give you.

Type A personality is a 'disorder' characterised by its sense of urgency in relation to time and by its readiness to show hostility. Individuals affected by this disorder are, in almost all cases, unaware they are suffering from it. They tend to believe that those who do not suffer from this distorted perception of time (which they argue is an adequate external manifestation of a highly responsible mind) are irresponsible, lazy, lacking ambition and unwilling to improve.

These specific personality traits are the symptoms of a very generalised disease of the conscience, which basically consists of a great affinity with an anxious search for power and dominion upon others. A thirst for leadership, protagonism, security, control, domination and the feeling of self-importance manifest as an incessant and indefatigable struggle. There is a constant need to acquire more and more material things, to participate in more and more events, in less and less time.

Modern psychologists and cardiologists label this group of symptoms as 'Personality Type A'. They believe it stems from a very well disguised insecurity about one's personal status or from great aggressiveness. I would say it arises most certainly from both of the above.

Insecurity and aggressiveness generates a struggle, that sooner or later gives birth to a new personality ingredient—the sense of urgency in its relationship to time—the 'hurry sickness'. Insecurity about personal status plus aggressiveness and a sense of urgency plus struggle result in a deep, and not always conscious, feeling of frustration. This in turn results in what is called 'free floating hostility'.

If the sufferer of the disorder is immersed for a long time in this senseless struggle, a struggle that generates frustration, a fifth component of this type of personality will appear. This component is characterised with a strong tendency to adopt self-destructive attitudes and habits.

If the individual's expectations are much higher than their actual achievements in everyday life their self-esteem will suffer considerable damage which only further accentuates insecurity. This can trigger a senseless and relentless struggle to acquire and accumulate possessions. Therefore, outwardly wearing the vestments of multiple external symbols that the sufferer sees as the unequivocal indicators of social and human status. Regardless of other opinions, if their personal expectations are higher than their achievements, their self-esteem will remain inadequate even though they might project the opposite image.

When those in charge of our upbringing, although well intentioned, try hard to instill in us a high and tenacious spirit of competition and instigate the desire to reach goals and objectives difficult to achieve, what they are actually doing is planting the seeds for unhappiness, frustration and bitterness. A child can feel very inadequate when an adult pats them on the back (very patronising), encouraging them to reach unreasonable goals while saying: 'It'll be awful if you cannot achieve that...', 'If I had your skills I would already...'.

Surrounding a child—or an adult—with irrational or inappropriate expectations in relation to their nature, while voicing the excuse of motivating them to succeed in life is the most successful way of planting, in a person, the feeling of failure. This implantation of fear is done while appearing to stimulate and nurture their ego i.e. 'You are so intelligent it would be a crime not to achieve it. So many mediocre people do, why not you?'

The lineal way of thinking which goes from left to right relates cause with first effect, second effect, third effect and so on, has led doctors, physiologist, anatomists and geneticists to believe this personality type is the result of a genetic predisposition. Psychiatrists, psychologists and sociologists assume Personality Type A is the outcome of the influence that our family's upbringing has had over us. They believe that our parents' particular perception system (the colour of the lens through which they saw the world, social and interpersonal relationships), have painted with different colours the perception we have of ourselves and others, as well as way in which we believe we must relate to them.

However, despite the fact that genetic predisposition, family and social atmosphere are very important factors which to some extent determine the final outcome of our personality, there are still many questions that sciences of genetics and sociology cannot answer. This lineal way of thinking raises many questions, Why do siblings with the same father and mother, brought up with the same value system, with the same encouragement and repression have different personalities?

Geneticists would argue that not all siblings have exactly the same chromosomal charge, except in the case of identical twins. It is worth noting that although identical twins have the same chromosomal charge, in a few cases they too have very different personalties.

It is my opinion that Personality Type A is primarily a disorder of the individual consciousness. This occurs prior to its incarnation, prior to its conception and it chooses the specific genetic map that will represent it with high fidelity. This type of personality uses the external frame of validation as an indicator of success. In modern industrialised countries where the frame of validation is found outside of ourselves this type of personality is becoming more and more common. As we look for external frames of reference, the Personality Type A is looking for models that they consider as very responsible, active, dynamic and competitive.

The borderline between a healthy dose of ambition and the traits of Personality Type A is sometimes subtle and hard to pin-point. In general, people with a healthy ambition are in possession of a powerful engine that drives them to improve their standard of living. They are always trying to make their homes more comfortable; to improve their physical, emotional, financial, social or academic health. But for them, comparing their achievements to those of others is irrelevant.

In contrast people suffering from an insane search for power, or from Personality Type A, compete in an aggressive way that not only involves the desire to win, but also the desire to dominate those they are trying to defeat. When dominating those they have defeated they also like to place them in an inferior position and to damage their self-esteem.

For the Personality Type A individual every competitor is a 'bastard' and the world is divided into winners and losers. Winners are those who belong to a higher social, and therefore, human status. Losers are those individuals belonging to a lower social and human status because they lack the testosterone needed to triumph—at least in the Type A's narrow concept of triumph.

Dr Meyer Friedman, the well-known cardiologist, founder of the Meyer Friedman Institute for the treatment of coronary patients, describes free floating hostility in people with type A personality as follows:

> 'It is a disguised and barely repressed fury that emerges quite frequently in response to trivial events, remaining undetected and unrecognised for a very long time. These individuals are very good at hiding, and always finding excuses and reasons for, their more or less permanent state of irritation. For example, when they snap furiously toward another driver, as a rule, the other is an idiot who has made an awful mistake. Queuing for a long time makes them furious, and, in their eyes rightly so, although everyone else observing the situation may condemn their tantrums. The resentment these individuals with type A personality have towards disrespectful youths listening to their "walkmans" in trains, buses or super-markets, seems to make sense; but sooner or later, even the

closest and more understanding friends of the hostile type A, begin to realise that he finds just too many reasons to become irate and that his reactions are far more intense than what the occasion calls for.

This hostility, of course, makes it very difficult for this kind of person to attract or accept pure affection. This happens because of the basic incompatibility between hostility and love. In this way, many type A individuals find it almost impossible to give or receive love graciously. Type A can give *loyalty*, can bring *humour*, can feel *worry*, but most often shuns any verbal expressions of human love—although they are capable of showering their pets with caresses and expressions of tenderness'.

This paradox of being able to love animals but not to express tenderness towards people is possible because for an aggressive competitive being, who is always in a hurry and searching for power, conceives love as a mathematical equation in which love equals submission, possession or obedience.

The type A personality tends to be strongly authoritarian and rigid. As time goes by these traits turn this individual into an intolerant being, hardly capable of accepting and adjusting to change. The eminently subjective sense of urgency (hurry sickness) these people usually suffer gives them airs of being important and scrupulously responsible.

All through their lives these individuals seem to be in the process of giving birth. Their time, unlike the time of those around them, which is irrelevant, is so important that it must never be wasted. They foster an insatiable need to carry out a large number of chores every day, of becoming involved in many events responds, in great measure, to the need to escape from themselves and to abort any initiative of abstract manifestation within their own mind which may lead to an enrichment of their inner life.

This might be the motive as to why type A personalities usually present with a well disguised and rationalised megalomania, airs of grandeur. It may be to justify to themselves how vital their special and subjective sense of urgency is, as well as their aggressiveness, their free floating hostility and the importance they place on the external world where their goals and objectives to succeed reside.

This relentless, senseless and anxious search for power and dominion, not only destroys relationships between husbands and wives, siblings, friends, partners and workmates but also results in an imbalance of their physical health. These individuals have a higher incidence of diabetes, high blood pressure, strokes, cardio-vascular disorders, migraines, hypercholesterolemia, multiple sclerosis, auto-immune disorders and other stress related maladies.

This is the reason such a destructive personality remains so well hidden and is often related to, and labelled as 'a strong and indomitable spirit.' Since childhood, we have been taught life is a struggle, and that to succeed in this struggle, enthusiasm is a vital ingredient. This may lead to two kinds of misconceptions:

Firstly, since the concept of struggle may easily be confused with the concept of fighting, those who take on life, as a fight, will live and grow fighting until there is no one else left to fight. This is the tragic fate of those unfortunate beings who end up fighting with their loneliness.

Secondly, 'impatient anxiety' may be confused with enthusiasm. Enthusiasm being the joy of doing our best which vibrates in harmony with our inner longings.

My concept of life is that it is not a struggle. Life is a wonderful and miraculous process of evolution, involving physical, mental, social and spiritual growth. Life is an adventurous and happy process of self-discovery giving us opportunities to learn. Life should be based on harmonious and co-operative relationships, instead of fight and competition.

There is an abysmal difference between type A and type B personalities; between the philosopher and the auditor, between a loving, tender, considerate spouse who is also a good mate and the person who believes a partner is a possession, an employee or just a provider. That is the difference between Jesus of Nazareth and Karl Marx, while the illuminated Son of Man preached equality for all men through the exaltation of the conscience, love and co-operation, the apologist of 'dialectic materialism' talks about the building of a perfect society founded on hatred and class struggle.

Within that intimate, but absolutely real connection between the body and the spirit, our spirit is the great leader (even when they mutually influence) and therefore our spirit is responsible for most of the success or failure of our body. In other words, within the spirit lies the responsibility for our illness or health. We may wonder: can our spiritual failures lead us to physical failures? It is obvious that people with type A personality (impatient, aggressive, competitive, seekers of status and intolerant) suffer more frequently of high blood pressure, arteriosclerosis, cerebral vascular strokes, high cholesterol, triglycerides, angina, coronary, diseases, heart attacks, stomach ulcers, migraine, Parkinson's disease. They also smoke more and have a harder time quitting.

As our need to grasp the intimate correlation between the changes in our organic chemistry and the legacy of our consciousness increases, the importance of super technical medicine devoid of philosophy will decrease. A medical-philosophical-spiritual movement will emerge that will become more vigorous with each passing day. Then, human quality and the great wisdom of the soul will be more appreciated in medical circles than the technical knowledge and possession of sophisticated electrical appliances doctors use nowadays to monitor the consequences of our spiritual problems.

The secret lies in living life with a special sense of mission, love and service, in which work performance, economic, social or academic acquisition stop being the indicators of success or failure.

ARTERIAL HYPERTENSION

'Conquering and handling the world: I have experienced that this fails. The world is a spiritual thing, which must not be handled. Whosoever handles it, destroys it. Whosoever wants to hold on to it, loses it.'

Lao Tze *The Tao Teh Ching*

I am sure almost every one of us at sometime in our lives, has taken a hose, connected it to a tap and watered the garden. We all understand that the water is under pressure inside the hose. Pressure is the force the running water exerts over each and every centimetre of the inside walls of the hose or tube through which it flows. The higher the pressure the stronger the ejection of the water, consequently the spurt of water will reach farther and cover a wider area. Some hoses have a device at the top end that allows the person to adjust the diameter of the orifice through which the water is ejected.

The tap to which the hose is connected always sends a uniform amount of water per unit of time, for example 0.5 litres per second. If the orifice's diameter, at the user end of the hose, is large the water will pour out under very little pressure and the gardener will only wet his feet. However, if the orifice is small the water will come out with increased force and speed in order to keep up with the same ejection rate of half a litre per second.

Something similar occurs with our body. Our heart is a miraculous organ that works as a suction and expulsion pump. It pumps our blood, with a specific force, into a system of conduits consisting of arteries, veins and capillaries. It then draws the blood back from our venous capillaries once it has delivered its oxygen cargo to each of our body's cells. The force and speed with which the blood moves inside our system will depend on the force and speed of the contraction and pumping of our heart and the resistance these conduits (hoses) will oppose.

A healthy vascular system, one with clean arteries, clear of fatty deposits on its internal walls, flexible and elastically malleable to the different changes in volume caused by waves in the blood stream, will give very little resistance to the blood wave sent by the heart, and be of great assistance in maintaining our blood pressure uniformity, even in the most remote corners of our body.

A vascular system made up of arteries that are 'rigid', 'fibrous', and 'strong' but 'inflexible' do not mould to the waves of the blood stream. The words in quotation marks will be later used to establish a relationship with the personality, perception system and nature of thought of the hypertensive type. Arteries of this type have their inner 'light'—their diameter—dimmed by deposits and 'fixations' of inflexible solid fat which blocks the blood stream, forcing the heart to pump harder. This results in a hypertrophy (increased volume) of the heart muscle, in order to increase its pumping force. The overall result is an escalation of pressure into the arteries.

If instead of thinking in a lineal way, we apply a metaphysical or vertical line of thinking and shift the description of the vascular system to the characteristics of two different types of personality we will observe the following. With a healthy and clean personality, clear of any deposits or 'fixations' of rigid concepts and prejudice, we find it is flexible and malleable to the changes by the different streams of thought; adaptable to changes in tradition that do not offend the very essence of eternal values and the pressure exercised from the outside world without struggle or resistance and without causing suffering, such as headaches or anguish.

On the other hand we will find with a rigid, fibrous and strong inflexible personality, that it is incapable of changing its way of thinking or its perception system to (widen its diameter) by adopting new concepts therefore its inner light, or diameter of understanding and tolerance is narrow. This personality type will keep the individual from enjoying anything different to itself, to its traditions and preferences. The pressure exercised by the outside world and society will seem gigantic, and the shadow of conflict will be forever present in those silent monologues that are constantly taking place in their mind.

Is it not really that hard to see that I am talking about one and the same superior reality—the conscience— manifesting itself simultaneously at two different levels. On the one hand at a mental/emotional level with its entire orchestra of negative or positive thoughts and emotions. And on the other hand, at a cardiovascular level through a hemodynamic process which may be either perfect or burdened with discomfort caused by the above mentioned mental/emotional influences.

The purpose of this book is to alert the reader to how physical health is only a reflection of the state of our conscience.

Nevertheless, it is only fair to say that any patient suffering from arterial hypertension (high blood pressure) must necessarily undergo regular checkups carried out by their doctor, since as their blood pressure increases so will the risk of heart attack, cerebrovascular accidents (brain haemorrhage, thrombosis, embolism or stroke).

I am not preaching against the use of pharmacological medication or any other therapeutic measure of conventional or alternative medicine. Medical remedies are extremely useful because they alleviate or eliminate symptomatic discomfort or pain. They therefore allow the patient, free of pain and at ease, to investigate their conscience's cause(s) of their complaint; something impossible to do while under the heavy weight of the symptomatic orchestra.

Approximately 3% of all cases of high blood pressure can be classified as secondary hypertension to some specific and identifiable pathology, for example: Cushings Syndrome, Aortic Constriction, Pheochromocytoma, etcetera. Some cases of transitory hypertension can be attributed to the use of certain medications, such as contraceptives, nasal decongestants, steroids and so on.

Of course in the case of secondary hypertension to an aortic constriction or a pheochromocytoma (a tumour that secretes a substance which increases blood pressure), the therapeutic priorities point to the surgical correction of the constriction or the extirpation of the tumour, after which this state of hypertension usually disappears. In cases of transitory hypertension caused by the ingestion or use of a certain medication or substance, since as its name indicates, it is only transitory, it will disappear once the substance in question has been eliminated from the system.

The great majority (95 to 97%) of cases of high blood pressure are classified as unspecific or idiopathic hypertension. Idiopathic is a nice little word doctors use to label all that they cannot explain to the patient and which, most probably, neither can we explain to ourselves.

Therefore, those who love power and control will have to learn to control not only the visible, explosive manifestations of their thoughts and emotions, but the very nature of these thoughts. This does not mean living in an environment bereft of stimulation, which could have an even worse result, it simply means transcending and transmuting the old way of thinking by adopting a new system of perception. This could have taken place in a spontaneous, free, conscious and joyful way, but instead it is forced on them through dis-ease and its consequent doses of suffering. In this way, the disease becomes a path to spiritual evolution. Every disease carries a teaching and if we study carefully what we should do, in order to improve our health we may discover what that message or teaching may by. Anything we were not ready to learn in a conscious and joyful way, we may have to learn because of a disease.

Regarding arterial hypertension, conventional medicine has frequently placed the responsibility on a word that is a little vague but sufficiently snobbish as to have become fashionable worldwide...stress. This word has the disadvantage of placing the cause of our complaints outside of ourselves. Maybe that's the reason doctors and their patients are so fond of it, since it exonerates the latter from their responsibility to change and provides the former with the opportunity to convert the word 'idiopathic' in something more recognisable. Once we realise that the root of our complaints lie in our own consciousness, our need of doctors and pharmaceuticals will gradually disappear.

Stress is not a cloud floating in the atmosphere that accidentally, or by fate, envelopes and takes possession of us. Stress is a state of mind, almost always fabricated by a system of defective thoughts and perceptions in our everyday interaction with our environment.

While it is true there are certain objective situations which are really stressful, capable of creating tension in the most phlegmatic individual, it is also true that the most stressed people are not those living under the most dangerous and miserable conditions. Stress is not so much related to the objective danger or misery of a given situation, as to the quantity and quality of the expectations we harbour, and the fear and frustrations these expectations create within ourselves.

Stress is fear. Stress is lack of love and acceptance. True love does not know fear. Stress is the ego disguised as concern. The ego is what distances us from unity and submerges us into separation and insecurity. Fear is not

Divine, it is diabolic and generates an incessant search for security, in this case power—he who is fearful believes power will bring him control, domination and security.

This chapter does not attempt to present a detailed description of all the chemical, hormonal, mechanical and physiological mechanisms leading to an idiopathic hypertension process. The fact that the term hypertension is preceded by the adjective 'idiopathic' already shows that neither doctors, physiologists nor 'scientific researchers' are knowledgeable of all the mechanisms involved. This is due to the obsessive tendency of lineal thinkers to look for physical causes as the origin of any physical manifestation.

This may be the reason why we still have a long list of diseases labelled 'idiopathic' because of the impossibility of finding an intimate physical-chemical mechanism that may satisfactorily explain the reason for its existence.

Another obsession worthy of mention is the compulsive tendency to brand a name on any behaviour that we perceive as abnormal. People demand a diagnosis! People love brands! People believe that if they have a name to call what they perceive as a problem, the perceived 'problem' vanishes (it is the origin of the over diagnosed ADHD, Asperger Syndrome, Autism, Dyslexia etcetera).

This chapter attempts to supply certain clues to help prevent the physical changes within the cardio-vascular system leding to hypertension in response to what we perceive, think, believe, feel and expect. If we hope to eradicate hypertension in future generations, the path will necessarily involve teaching our children not to worship power and success, but rather to praise an attitude of service to others in tolerance and love. We need to teach our children to enjoy the entire journey and not to place the greatest emphasis on the results they've achieved.

The patient with hypertension must not abandon his pharmacological treatment or checkups while pursuing a change in their basic patterns of thought. A change in which they start enjoying what they do, the way they do it, for the sake of what they are doing, independent of results. A change in which the most relevant thing becomes the journey involved in searching for their goal and not the goal itself!

To end this chapter, I would like to leave you with the message of a Jewish Rabbi, a psychiatrist named Harold Kushner, who wrote a wonderful book titled, *When All You Have Ever Wanted is Not Enough*. It is a passage which re-affirms my personal opinion that those we consider 'strong' people (who love power, wealth, to be in command and have control), are prone to high blood pressure, heart attacks, cerebrovascular accidents and loneliness in old age. They are also sad and lonely people, alone even when they can be wealthy, for the exercising of power may bring about adulation, but never love; and only those who love us will be with us in the last leg of our journey.

Dr Harold Kushner writes: 'That the search for wealth and power and the exercising of this power tends to separate us from our fellowman. Many are driven by it, not only to take up life in competition instead of cooperation, which makes it difficult for them to relate to others. If you love someone only because he/she is forever trying to please you, that is not love, but an indirect way of loving yourself. Power, like water, emanates from above and flows down towards someone below you. Love only happens between two people who consider themselves equal and satisfy each other. If one commands and the other obeys we could have, in the best of cases, loyalty and gratitude, but not love. An isolated human being is not a human being. We cannot be truly human in isolation. The virtues that make us human only emerge through our relationship with our fellowman.

The real hell is that, in our vehement persistence to reach success, we have deteriorated our relationship with others to a point that we only see them in the light of the benefits they could offer us. The possibility of dominating others (employees, friends, children, siblings or parents) may be temporarily gratifying, but in the long run condemns us to loneliness, since reliable, long lasting company comes from love. Love and power are incompatible! God shows a particular preoccupation with the poor and those who suffer, and certain misgivings toward the rich; not because it is good to be poor and immoral to be rich, but because the poor and the suffering seem to have a greater need of others. In general terms, they are more vulnerable and less arrogant, all of which constitutes a profoundly human trait.'

CHOLESTEROL

'Meditation is the process of letting go of what we think we know, and opening up to questions that appears to be obvious.'

Graham Williams, *Insight and Love*

'In most love relationships the presence of an active will is disruptive and dangerous. Wilfulness that arises from disappointment or from pure selfishness detracts from love.'

Sam Reifler, *The I Ching*

Cholesterol has become a topic of worrying relevance at the present time. The high incidence of arteriosclerosis, arterial hypertension, coronary artery disease, angina pectoris, myocardial infarction, cerebrovascular accidents and the entire pathological orchestra of arterio-sclerosis and atero-sclerosis (fat deposits on arterial walls), has turned the word cholesterol into a much feared and over used term of a frightening phantom. Also it is a great topic for conversation, the symbol of high social status for some and poor health for others: 'My Doctor placed me on a diet, because I need to lower my cholesterol levels,' is something we frequently hear from a friend at a social gathering.

What is Cholesterol?

This book was not written for medical specialists, but rather for average individuals, like you and I. It is for all of us who walk the streets with our big or small backpacks overflowing with worries, plans, dreams, hopes, requited or unrequited love. For this reason I will try, as far as possible, to demystify the terminology, making use of examples to facilitate an understanding of the topic. However, we will need to take a roundabout route before we reach 'cholesterol'.

Greasy and fatty substances are made up of long chains of carbon atoms, from nine to eighteen carbon atoms aligned one after the other. Every carbon atom has four valencies. Placed in a row, each of these atoms will exchange and use up one of its valencies to remain joined to the atom immediately behind it and in front of it. The atom will still have two remaining free valencies to saturate; each taking an atom of hydrogen (hydrogen has only one valency). Subsequently, because there is no other atom behind, in the case of the first carbon atom, or in front, in the case of the last one, those at each end of the chain will be left with an extra valency. This valency will also saturate with another atom.

All these carbon atoms in the chain with the two extra valencies (the valencies not used to form a chain) saturated with hydrogen, are *saturated fats*. But if one carbon atom uses two of its valencies, instead of one to join the next carbon atom (disregarding a hydrogen atom), we will have a chain with a double joint at some point and a missing hydrogen atom. This chain is, therefore, *not saturated*, and we call this fat *mono unsaturated*, since one of its atoms is not saturated with hydrogen. If it has two or more of its atoms using two of their valencies to join the next atom, then we talk of *polyunsaturated fats*.

Saturated fats all tend to solidify. Mono and polyunsaturated fats remain fluid even at very low temperatures and for easy identification we shall call them oils. Lard and butter (saturated fatty acids) are hidden in almost all animal derived food, while oils (mono and polyunsaturated fatty acids) are present mainly in vegetable foods.

Saturated fatty acids solidify and gelatinise to the point they can be cut with a knife or scooped with a spoon. When heated to a high temperature (above 85°C) they melt and become fluid. Once ingested and assimilated, they solidify inside our system becoming part of our adipose (fatty) membrane or infiltrating the walls of our arteries. They form blocks that impede blood circulation, adding to the risk of thrombosis and embolism that can affect any organ in our body.

Cholesterol is an ester of saturated fatty acids acting as an alarm announcing the risks of possible thrombi-embolic accidents. Its close link to arteriosclerotic processes is doubtless, as is the role of saturated fat acids in the origin of fatty deposits infiltrating the arteries walls (atheroma).

Once formed, it is very difficult to eliminate these fatty deposits, since their melting point is above 85°C Degrees. There are substances that can reduce the melting point of cholesterol and other fatty acids involved in forming deposits. Vitamin E (Alpha Tocopherol) reduces their melting point to approximately 50°C degrees. This figure is still very high, for our body cannot cope with a body temperature of such magnitude. A temperature above

40°C degrees and over brings about convulsions and delirium. Therefore, not even a regime of intense and prolonged physical exercise will eliminate the fat infiltrated among the different layers of the artery wall. But an appropriate combination of vitamin E and Lecithin reduces the melting point to below the normal body temperature, making elimination so much easier.

In an integral arterial wall it appears to be very difficult that deposits of fatty acids can take place. When the arterial wall has a tear due to an elevation of the blood pressure combined with a loss of flexibility, platelets attach to it in order to avoid any widening of the artery. This small mound of platelets facilitates the accumulation of fatty material. As a consequence arterial integrity is a significant factor in the genesis of atheroma. Vitamin C, bioflavonoids, anti-oxidants, folic acid and colloidal minerals appear to play a significant role in avoiding the atheroma formation and even in dissolving if one already exists.

Vegetable oils remain fluid even at low temperatures, so there is no risk of atheroma formation. The mere presence of mono, or polyunsaturated fatty acids interferes with their solidification and impedes other fats from depositing within the arteries.

Someone once said that people are as old as their arteries; this assertion is strongly backed by logic. Clean and flexible arteries guarantee good irrigation and oxygenation of our brain, lung, renal system, glandular system, muscle and other bodily tissues, ensuring our bodily functions are kept at an optimum level.

Endocrinologists believe we are as old as our glands, which also has a solid basis. A healthy efficient glandular system keeps the human machine well oiled and toned. However, our internal secretion glands (thyroid, pituitary, reproductive, pancreas etc) cannot adequately function without proper blood circulation and its corresponding oxygenation. Dieticians and nutritionists assure us that, 'we are what we eat'. This assertion, also has some basis since our external appearance partly depends on the quantity and quality of the foods we consume. Nutrition and diet are an important factor in gaining or losing physical fitness, as well as improving or deteriorating the good working order of our organs.

Also we are what we believe we think and we feel we are. What we think or feel will determine what we eat, how often we exercise, in which field we'll work, our family and social relationships, our preferences, the aim of our life and so on.

There are people who continue to have high cholesterol levels even after a very long time on a specially designed diet intended to lower it. Some, despite taking pharmaceutical remedies to accelerate the elimination process, persist with almost unchanged levels. Physiologists explain this by the fact that the liver is capable of producing its own cholesterol. But why do some livers produce more cholesterol than others? Geneticists will reply it happens because there is a gene, found in some people, carrying a specific 'message' that causes their liver to produce more cholesterol than the average.

Message? Are we talking about thought and will? Are genetic messages and information the vital elements of thought and will? Are genetic messages, in regard to the mental process, what the atom is to the solar system? Are our genes capable of mutation? Is our thought pattern a force that stimulates mutation? Who deposited this information and these messages in our genes? If we keep receding in our footsteps somewhere along the line we will reach the conclusion that some kind of consciousness did. The core of genetic messages lies at a consciousness level!

When we change our perception, our way of thinking and our feelings automatically change as well. This change will cause considerable alterations in our blood chemistry which in turn affects the metabolism of our cells. Where then lies the steering wheel of our cell's metabolism? Where then lies the problem?

Solving the problem of having hypercholesterolemia requires a change in our perception system, our thoughts, our feelings and our values. A spontaneous adoption of the appropriate lifestyle will follow this change which, if maintained for a long enough time, will ultimately result in alterations to genetic messages and information.

It's surprising to see how some centenarians keep mentally lucid and physically agile, enjoying not only more years in their lives, but also more life in their years. Many of us harbour an intense fear of old age, possibly because we partly relate it to the total loss of our self-sufficiency. We assume that being old represents an end to our sexual activities, a loss of control of our sphincters, immobility, and an inability to defend ourselves from an ever more aggressive and disrespectful youth, memory loss and the inability to think coherently.

Although it is true that there are certain genetic factors determining the age at which each of these complaints will emerge, it is also true that an appropriate lifestyle and an adequate system of perception and thoughts retards the establishment of these complaints even within individuals who are genetically predisposed to them.

We can ingest cholesterol in our foods, especially animal products. We can produce cholesterol from glycerides and steroids ingested also with our food. Our body can also manufacture cholesterol (mainly via our liver) through complex chemical-enzymatic processes. Our genetic background, our pattern of emotional response and pattern of behaviour predetermine the efficiency of these processes.

Once cholesterol has made its appearance and is circulating in our blood stream, it will join, in some cases, with plasmic lipoproteins. If it joins plasmic lipoproteins of a high molecular density (HMD), it will be used as a source of energy, metabolise and then be eliminated. If it adheres to plasmic lipoproteins of a low molecular density (LMD), cholesterol will be deposited on any tear of the arterial wall in which platelets have already started accumulating. The fatty material will take on the role of cement and the platelets will be the bricks. We already know the consequences.

An intimate knowledge of this process brings us to the conclusion that even more important than the quantity of fat we ingest, is the quality of these fats, and the type of proteins with which we accompany them with in our daily eating.

Of course the consumption of saturated fats will increase the level of cholesterol and its tendency to deposit it in the arteries. For this reason this type of fatty acids has been linked to heart and blood circulation diseases. Given that these animal fats contain high percentages of saturated fatty acids, its consumption increases the risk of arteriosclerosis.

Some historic religious books have already illustrated knowledge of the risk associated with eating animal fats. In the Old Testament of the Bible, Leviticus 7:22-26, states: 'And the Lord spoke unto Moses, saying: Speak unto the children of Israel saying: Ye shall eat no manner of fat, of ox, or of sheep, or of goat. And the fat of the beast shall dieth of itself, and the fat of that which is torn by beasts may be used in any other use, but ye shall not eat of it. For whosoever eateth the fat of the beast, which man offer in offering made by fire unto the Lord, even the soul that eateth it shall be cut off from his people. Moreover, ye shall eat no manner of blood, whether it be of fowl, or of beast, in any of your dwellings.'

We also find references in the Bible to the doctrine of vegetarianism in Genesis 3:18, 'And thou shalt eat the herb of the field.' And 3:19, 'In the sweat of your face shalt thou eat bread, till thou return unto the ground;

for out of it wast thou taken; for dust thou art, and unto dust shalt thou return.'

I believe it is not possible to maintain low cholesterol levels with temporary measures. One needs to adopt a permanent determined lifestyle brought about by an awakening of our consciousness. This awakening of consciousness will release us from preconceived ideas born from family, social, national, ethnic and cultural conditioning. It will be an awakening of consciousness dissolving fixed conceptions and feelings of identity which blind and prevent us from visualising the many possibilities of any specific situation.

People suffering from high levels of cholesterol are people who react to situations in a very predictable way, that is, they always react in the same manner to the same type of event. They have a strong sense of identity and are attached to a culturally conditioned perception system which drowns all other options.

Perhaps the first step in reducing cholesterol is to learn to meditate, letting go of what we think we know, and open ourselves to question that appear to be obvious.

DEMENTIA

He had his glance so long, as a stutterer's
    compliment.
He sat down on the bench beholding the hills so
    far away.
His mind was creeping silently
Through a field of aromatic nostalgia.
And that face... that face!
Usually inexpressive began glowing with the light
That in the morning filters
Between dewdrops suspended from leaves.
It appeared that this old man, so tired,
Who walked with scuffling feet,
The moment he sat down on the solitary park
    bench
Under the influence of one silent spell,
Transformed his tiredness and sadness
Into an explosion of renewed rapture.
I never knew, during that time,
If the magic sprouting from his eyes
The moment he looked at the hills so far away,
Was magic born from the breeze, the view or the
    environment?
Or if it was joy piercing
From within, through the window of his eyes.

Sergio Prado-Arnuero

This chapter has been constructed, as have all chapters in this book, with the purpose of supporting my strongly held view that, our state of health, or ill health, is a legacy of our consciousness. That possibility, all clinical syndromes are only the outward manifestation of an underlying state of consciousness.

Dementia is the loss of intellectual functions such as memory, thought and reasoning, sufficiently severe to interfere with a person's daily living. It is not a disease in itself, but a group of symptoms accompanying some other illness or physical conditions...but are they really physical?

The cause and pace of the development of dementia varies. Probably the best known diseases capable of producing dementia are: Alzheimer's, Parkinson's, multiple brain strokes, Huntingdon's, Pick's and Crentzfeldt Jakob's disease.

There are some conditions that may cause or imitate dementia. Conditions such as depression, brain tumours, cranium-encephalic trauma, hydrocephalous, infectious diseases like AIDS, meningitis, syphilis, alcoholism (Korsakoff Dementia) and problems of the thyroid gland. *Principles Of Internal Medicine* Harrison's 10th Edition

Alzheimer's Disease

This disease is the most common cause of dementia. It is a progressive degenerative disorder which attacks the brain provoking disorders in memory, thought and behaviour. The first most obvious symptom of this disease is a gradual loss of memory. Sufferers start to forget the names of friends or the place where they left their keys and often blame relatives when something goes missing. They forget to mail letters they have written and may believe that they have already done so. They forget the order of putting on their clothes going out with their underwear over their outfits, or have their shoes on the wrong foot. Frequently they forget addresses and easily become disorientated getting lost in areas where they have lived and visited for years. They can even get lost in their own home, forget to eat, or else eat and forget they have, or wander aimlessly through the streets much to the anxiety and grief of their loved ones.

Their sphincters become affected losing efficiency and they become incontinent both anally and vesically because their sphincter muscles lack tone and loose their capacity to contract. Or is it that they forget to tighten them enough to retain the urine and faeces until the appropriate time? Is this just the sphincter manifestation of a, 'this doesn't bother me, this doesn't affect me, this has nothing to do with me' attitude?

In this respect, one can also ask the question: does a gradual and persistent loss of memory bring about a gradual and persistent disinterest in life, family and the world? Or is it that this lack of interest and motivation brings them, as the logical sequence, to the escape route of loosing touch with reality through the slow and steady loss of memory?

What was the individual degree of 'joyful acceptance' of changes brought about by the inevitable passage of time in their environment? Did the individual accept with genuine joy the natural limitations of their age? Through what perception system did the individual see the changing world around them? What kind of expectations did the individual nourish regarding their spouse, children, grandchildren, socio-economic status and sexual life? What interest does the world hold for the individual, when they feel it no longer is the world they once loved? What interest does the individual have in living in this world, when they believe it isn't what it used to be and it will never be again?

In their notable and progressive decline in skills to carry out routine chores; in their disorientation regarding time and space; in their confused judgment; in the evident changes to their personalities; in their difficulties with learning and in their loss of verbal and communication skills, don't we incidentally see it as an effective escape route from a reality that for some time, or perhaps all of their lives, they have perceived as highly unpleasant and threatening?

We like to believe that aluminium intoxication is to blame for Alzheimer's disease. It is not my intention to deny the role of aluminium in the pathogenesis of this disease. If we refer to another cause of dementia, Korsakoff's, alcohol seems to be the culprit. However, beneath the alcohol consumption we find an addictive personality. This personality precedes any cerebral damage caused by an intensive and prolonged ingestion of alcohol. In Alzheimer's disease this connection is not always so easy to detect.

As with all other kinds of dementia the pace and development of Alzheimer's disease varies from case to case. The collapse of a victim to Alzheimer's may take up to twenty years or longer from the time of onset of the symptoms. Eventually, the disease leaves the individual totally unable to look after him or herself. This consequently, may lead to severe, or fatal accidents or even death from starvation or by neglect from those who care for them. Are they perhaps deep down seeking this?

Confirming the diagnosis of this disease is only possible through the examination of brain tissue, something usually done during an autopsy. It is important that any patient showing symptoms of dementia undergoes an examination, since approximately 20% of cases initially suspected of having Alzheimer's disease prove to have other causes. These 20% of cases can be treated and reversed through conventional therapeutic measures.

Could it be that these reversals respond to a change of mentality, or to a change of their emotional make up?

Multiple Stroke-Induced Dementia

This is a kind of dementia resulting from the death of brain tissue due to cerebral bleeds and anoxia. The onset of symptoms may be relatively sudden due to the fact that there may be a series of small asymptomatic (without symptoms) stroke bleeds that manifest in an abrupt way. These strokes may damage certain areas of the brain responsible for specific functions, which may produce general symptoms of dementia. As a result, this kind of dementia can imitate Alzheimer's disease.

This type of dementia is not reversible or curable but detection of any underlying condition, such as high blood pressure, high levels of cholesterol and triglycerides, type A personality etcetra, usually leads to specific treatment which may alter the development of the condition. Stroke-induced dementia is generally diagnosed through a clinical, physical, neurological examination and radiology techniques. Techniques such as computerised tomography, magnetic resonance imaging help identify those affected areas of the brain.

I believe all the borders separating the different diseases capable of causing dementia are artificial. In fact, once the picture of dementia is completely pieced together with all its symptomatic orchestra, there is little or no difference between them.

Parkinson's Disease

This is a progressive disease of the central nervous system (CNS) that, in the United States alone, affects more than 11 million people. Sufferers of this disease lack a substance called Dopamine which is used by the Central Nervous System to control muscular activity.

Parkinson's disease is characterised by a slight shaking of the hands (specially the thumb, index and middle fingers), a stiffness of the limbs and joints, speech impediment and difficulty in initiating physical movement. The picture is complicated in the advanced stages of the disease usually with the onset of Alzheimer's. Additionally, some Alzheimer's patients also develop Parkinson's disease.

When checking the symptomatology of fear, the effects vary depending on the degree of the fear felt. Panic, for example, is characterised by agitation, tremor and anxiety. Terror has a deeper degree of fear than panic and produces varying degrees of paralysis, difficulties with, or an absence of speech, extreme rigidity, paleness, generalised weakness and lose of sphincter control. Strong wilful individuals when trying to overcome or disguise a terror state may suffer a transient syndrome identical to Parkinson's.

Individuals who are used to dominating others or enjoying the spotlight, become secretly terrified with the possibility of losing the attention of the public; of being in the spotlight and of loosing control. Does the medical tendency of placing bio-chemical brain imbalance as a cause for emotional states, and never the emotional states as the cause of brain bio-chemical imbalances stop us from getting the right answer?

Many people believe that 'Mohammed Ali' developed Parkinson's as a consequence of his profession, in particular the frequent head blows that provoked numerous micro brain injuries. Was it Mohammed Ali's fear of losing his punching precision that resulted in the first physical manifestation of his disease, his constant hand shaking (the tools of his precision)?   Could the fear of losing his 'butterfly floating' movements be the underlying cause of the stiffness of his limbs and joints? Could the fear of losing his speed of movement now create difficulties in initiating them?   Could the fear of losing his loquacity create in Mohammed Ali his speech impediment?

I personally feel that his disease could be due to his gigantic ego and his intense fear of waiting for the arrival of his unavoidable decay and withdrawal from the spotlight. Fear may have so absorbed him that the temporary successful attempts to mask this terror and their external manifestations erupted one day with the onset of Parkinson's. Perhaps one day researchers will look at the relationship between fear/terror and the blood Dopamine levels prompting them to create the pill to overcome fear (another quick fix)!

This brings us back to this book's central theme—to demonstrate that all diseases share a common mental-spiritual-emotional root. In the case of dementia, I believe that even when it is the consequence of diseases such as Alzheimer's, Parkinson's, cerebro-vascular accidents (stroke), alcoholism or depression there is a pre-established way of thinking, of perceiving the world and life in general. Are these pre-established ways of thinking and perception what cause the chronic fear and the latent depression, which after a long time generate the permanent physical changes that pave the path for dementia?

The world belongs to the mental plane. The events of the outside world affect each and every one of us in a totally different way depending on how we see, judge and perceive them according to our thoughts, values and beliefs. We perceive the world according to the colour of the lenses we use when looking at it. Our thoughts and judgments create emotions and feelings of happiness, satisfaction, joy and ecstasy, or frustration, resentment and ire or fear. We may see the world as a beautiful place where life is a wonderful experience worthy of being lived fully, or we may see it as a battlefield, a chamber of grief and torture. Either way, it is the same world. The only difference is the lense though which we choose to view it.

We may see life as a painful and miserable chain of misfortunes from which, consciously or subconsciously we seek to escape. Escape? How?

Through alcoholism, drug addiction, traffic or firearm accidents, suicide, euthanasia, workoholism, TV addiction or the loss of memory and contact with reality.

Pre-established or preconditioned concepts about life, relationships, marriage, family, friendship, success, failure and love do not help us to perceive life in all its splendour. In order for us to appreciate life and everything it has to offer us, it will be necessary for us to strip ourselves of these concepts and expectations and to open our hearts to every experience without feeling the need for branding them. In this way we will learn that problems and disease are opportunities— marvellous opportunities—for us to rediscover our life's mission, or at the very least, our spirituality.

An extremely competitive society is not a desirable place for fragile people or for those who believe they have outlived their usefulness. These people must rediscover their sense of mission and realise that no matter what their age; no matter what their state of health; no matter what their financial position, there is always someone who would appreciate a fragment of their time; their company, an ear prepared to listen to them and a hand prepared to give warmth. Overcoming dementia is to overcome our own fears and expectations.

ALCOHOL AND DRUGS

'Whosoever knows others is clever,
Whosoever knows himself is wise.
Whosoever conquers others has force.
Whosoever conquers himself is strong.
Whosoever asserts himself has will-power.'

Lao Tze *The Tao Teh Ching*

It seems paradoxical that in this era of technological discovery and advancement many of us still know very little about our own mind and body. We know little about the way in which our body and mind relates to our surroundings; all with which we come into direct or indirect contact; everything that manages to penetrate our tissues and may alter our body functions; our sphere of knowledge; our behaviour and our state of mind.

You will not find in this chapter a minute description of all the developmental mechanisms and phenomena relating to the tolerance of, and dependency upon, alcohol and drugs as there are a wide variety of books dealing with this already. This chapter addresses what I believe are the foundations from which sprout alcoholism and drug addiction.

Those who have not felt the scourge of these substances on themselves or family members may think this chapter is irrelevant to their life. However, we live in a society that actively pollutes not only its external environment (atmosphere, land, lakes, rivers and seas) but also our personal internal environment (blood, other bodily fluids, the air inside our lungs and brain tissue). Therefore, any discussion about the use of alcohol and other drugs becomes a very relevant topic.

Today we are witnessing the birth and growth of a planetary and probably cosmic consciousness. A consciousness that teaches us that we are all voyagers and crew on an eternal space sojourn, all travelling aboard the spaceship *Planet Earth*. Today, when each person's fate is linked to everyone else's, and the destiny of humankind depends on the integrity and first-class functioning of this worldly spaceship we also must look at our own personal vehicle and the sick, irresponsible and artificial contamination to which we are submitting our bodies, minds and souls.

A drug is a substance which when entering the body through any route alters the body's physiological functions. It affects mainly the brain and the Central Nervous System modifying the state of our mind, behaviour, perception, reactions to external stimuli and our processes of thought.

Drugs alter our perception of reality in such a way that many use them in a desperate search to escape the reality they are experiencing. Drugs do not alter reality itself, only the way reality is perceived while the effects last. Drug use results in bringing about a very unpleasant aftermath which ends up reinforcing the stress or depressive state the drug's user was attempting to eliminate. This result provokes the repeated self-administration of the drug in doses progressively higher and with increased frequency, developing a psychological dependency. I will not endeavour to explain here physical dependency it is just sufficient to point out that each drug has its own neuro-chemical and enzymatic process for the development of its physical dependency, and tolerance.

All those involved in studies of the drug addiction phenomenon: doctors; psychologists; sociologists and moralists view the problem from different angles leading them to use different language, to formulate different conclusions and seek different paths of treatment and solution. Depending on the way it is addressed, as well as the language and the solution adopted, we may talk of a medical, psychological, sociological or moral model for drug or alcohol misuse. Such a division, otherwise artificial, helps us understand the whole, while studying each part separately. Each of these parts requires the adoption of different approaches to a solution.

Doctors believe drug addiction is a consequence of a combination of factors; one being an inherited genetic predisposition provoking a brain chemical imbalance responsible for the addiction illness. In this instance, the addicted person is a victim of the toxic effects of the drug in a previously vulnerable and imbalanced brain. The patient is not therefore responsible for his or her illness due to the fact that they were born with a failure created in the human factory, the human geno-pool. Of course the medical model's solution—a pharmacological one—is the 'quick fix' that never has fixed anything. Medication is used in order to neutralise and minimise the harm caused by the drug. However, this model not only releases the individual from any responsibility but also disempowers them to the extent that they loose their decision-making options. When we remove responsibility we are also removing hope. If the problem is caused by a gene then it follows that the individual can do little themselves to prompt change? Removing hope disempowers the drug abuser while empowering the doctor and those who supply prescribed drugs.

To the moralist the solution lies in the punishment and the educational re-enforcement of ethically moral values. The sociologist blames the problem on poverty, unemployment and residential overcrowding and sees the solution in minimising the gap between social strata or in a war against poverty. The psychologist believes the solution lies in psychological support and individual or group psychotherapy to overcome the basic addictive personality leading the drug user/abuser to shift their addiction to interpersonal relationships, work, sport, and so on.

We as human beings are 'Bio–Psycho–Social–Spiritual' entities (not spelt in order of importance) and the way we address the problem of drug addiction—or any other problem affecting us—should be a holistic, integral, totalitarian approach. A medical, psychological, moral, educational and sociological approach coordinated under a gigantic worldwide campaign, since it's a worldwide problem, would enable us to build a strong barrier to contain the problem. Personally, I believe the final touch, and probably the most important in the fight against drugs is to address issues of spirituality.

Perhaps the process of civilisation with its inherent technological advancement has gradually generated a spiritual vacuum in the entire world. It is this process of civilisation that has divested doctors of their priestly character and priests of their medical character. It has also substituted the verbalising of love and respect towards parents, elders, others and the self as television, the internet and high-tech games encourage a fanatical admiration; idolatry of performers; unrealistic families and false heroes as they bombard us with bottled stereotypes of sexual eroticism or the illusion of military, economic and political power.

Western civilisation has its own fanaticism as radical as that of any eastern ideology and we export it via radio and television, videos and movies to the rest of the planet. We behave in a very expansionist and invasive way without any consideration to the traditions and beliefs of other cultures. Then we wonder, why do they hate us?

Our civilisation is creating android beings, apparently human, but devoid of spirituality. This kind of void generates a desperate search for a sense of identity and belonging in order to reaffirm the self-esteem of someone who has been robbed of their many possessions, but essentially the most precious of all...their Spirituality.

Many humans lack a sense of identity, belonging and love, which may assist in developing drug addiction. The problem is not genetic or bio-chemical, it happens because the individual is desperately searching for the elements of identity, belonging and love outside themselves. Society and the educational system foster the belief that our feelings of identity must be sourced in the stiff concepts of nationality, language, religion, race, social status and culturally conditioned customs and expectations. Addictive personalities become nourished from the frustrations and feelings of inadequacy born from an expectation of success or the tendency to use an external frame of reference from which they are evaluated.

In the past Alchemists looked for the 'Philosophical Stone' that supposedly could turn ordinary metals into gold. The Spaniards went crazy when they reached America in their search for El Dorado. The Crusaders risked lives, homes and kingdoms in their quest for the Holy Sepulchre and the Holy Grail. Dr Faust, by Goethe, signed a deal with the Devil, and Ecclesiastes had it all and conquered all without ever discovering the 'meaning of life'.

Today, humans are desperately searching for this 'meaning'. They continue searching for El Dorado, the Philosophical Stone, the Holy Sepulchre and the Holy Grail in alcohol, psychodelic inducing drugs, ecstasy, speed, faster cars, violent music, sex as well as economic, social and political power. They also look for it in the stereotype relationships portrayed by the mass media, in take away love and sex, in computer games or in the violence from sport stadiums.

However, the real Philosophical Stone, meaning, El Dorado, Holy Sepulchre and the Holy Grail are inside us. There is no Messiah. If someone tells you he is the Christ, flee from him. If someone swears to be the

Buddha, don't listen to him. The real Messiah does not dwell in Rome, Guyana, Waco, Japan or India. The real Messiah is not a priest or guru. The real Messiah is in the soul of each and every one of us.

We are spirits having a human experience. We are Gods pretending to be naïve! The legacy of our consciousness is Divine! We lose what we inherently possess by not appreciating it. That is why we succumb to illness, because we lack self-awareness, self-love, self-knowledge and therefore self-esteem. The role of our identity is to compromise or to come to terms with ourselves, with our spirit and therefore with life itself. We need to revere life and the first life we need to revere is the life that is within us.

Heaven is not a place located in a particular point in space. Heaven is not a time. Heaven is a state of consciousness with a corresponding state of mind. Light, colours, sounds, are only ways of perceiving movement. If our state of consciousness changes, everything around us changes. When someone is in love, we say he sees the world in a 'rosy colour'. Heaven is being in love with life, with the universe, with one's self and their function and role within the cosmic play.

Heaven is Love. No one can sell us Heaven in a wine bottle, or rolled in a cigarette of tobacco, or in a marijuana joint, or concentrated in Angel powder (cocaine), or inside a syringe of heroine, or in a dose of lysergic acid (LSD). Through drugs we can have a glimpse of life in other dimensions, but the return becomes more painful each time. We have our own internal mechanism to attain Heaven in a stable and durable way, but these mechanisms are based on self-awareness, self-esteem, love of the world, reverence towards life and a joyful acceptance of our reality.

Likewise we cannot find Heaven in television programs as they only fulfil a recreational role. However, intentional or not, they do instill in us stereotypes that are totally removed from our reality. They increase the level of basic eroticism forcing the viewer to make adjustments between their own reality and that of the television program. The search for intense relationships and emotions becomes an obsession.

These stereotypes of physical beauty imposed by cinema and television are anything but natural. I am not opposed to physical beauty or personal care. I want to point out that for a housewife giving love and care to her husband, children, siblings, mother and other family members, it is impossible to keep up with world affairs let alone compete with these professional and artificual stereotypes.

Alcohol and drug problems are a problems of consciousness. They are problems linked to a lack of love linked to our perception system and our expectations. We cannot blame society as if it were something above and apart of us, since society is the product of ourselves. We are not just spectators in the social drama. Even when domineering races, social classes and cultures hold the power of the mass media, we still have the power of our own consciousness. So what right do we have to complain when we are active participants in society. After all, the social consciousness of a large group of people is simply the sum of its individual consciousness.

Society as a whole may be at fault but alcohol and drug abusers are not passive victims of the social contract, they also have their quota of responsibility since their addiction is a deviation of their own consciousness. When a large group of us choose this path it is because we are all going in the wrong direction. We have not offered a viable alternative to the drug addicted and he/she in turn, refuses to look for one.

When our perception and value system enables us to reject the unreal and instead admire people such as Mahatma Gandhi, Martin Luther King Jr, Mother Teresa of Calcutta, St Francis of Assisi, and others who give of themselves or risk their lives to protect us, we will be close to overcoming the addictive personality.

AGING

'Man when he enters life, is soft and weak; when he dies, he is hard and strong. Plants, when they enter life are soft and tender; when they die they are hard and stiff. Therefore, the hard and strong are companions of death, the soft and weak are companions of life.'

Lao Tze *The Tao Teh Ching*

Currently, human life expectancy in developed countries (industrialised countries) is around seventy-five years. However, there is a slight difference of three or four years in favour of females. This means that women live for an average of seventy-seven years and men between seventy-three and seventy-four. Twenty years ago this difference was eight to ten years, a figure that has progressively lessened as the female population has changed in mind and spirit. This change has brought about changes in their sphere of emotions, expectations, eating habits, use of alcohol, tobacco and other drugs and in their inter-action with others even in the way and speed at which they drive a car.

In our society, to reach and to pass the eighty-year barrier is proof of longevity. To be over ninety is considered a feat that becomes a real luxury if, at this age one can still walk without aid, control bladder and intestine evacuations and if one is still mentally lucid.

How often do we hear the young say they do not wish to reach old age, because old age is horrible? They think and talk this way for two reasons:

1) They hear their elders complain about being old. 'Oh my son, how terrible it is to be old!' is a common phrase among older individuals who, for different motives, don't love their current phase of life. This may have more to do with their particular family and social situation than with the aging process itself.

2) They believe all those who approach, or pass, ninety years must be, unavoidably, unable to fend for themselves, either relegated to a wheelchair or unable to move about without the aid of a walking frame and suffering from incontinence and having memory loss to the point of not being able to recognising their closest relatives. They see themselves as speaking incoherently as they mix, without any sense or order, memories with real or imaginary events.

Reaching one hundred years of age enjoying physical and mental good health is not only a luxury and a feat but a rarity which is being more frequently observed in first world countries. There is medical and anthropological evidence to justify the belief that humans are designed to live between one hundred and twenty and one hundred and forty years.

In 1991 in Oakland, California, the media reported the death of a local resident named Arthur Reed who was one hundred and twenty-four years of age. In Azan Japan, Shigechiyo Isumi passed away in February 1986, aged one hundred and twenty-one. I was pleased to have had the acquaintance of someone living in Parramatta, a hero of the First World War who was already ninty-eight when I commenced writing this book. At that time he was full of energy, mentally lucid and had a great joy of living. Such longevity leads us to consider that what is possible for some may be possible for all.

We often hear people, who insist on making a myth of the past, arguing that the generations preceding us were stronger and lived longer. I'll remind these people that in the time of the Roman Caesars human life expectancy was around twenty-five years. At the beginning of the twentieth century the average life-span increased in relation to the decrease in the number of deaths at and during childbirth.

However, despite all achievements in lowering infant mortality we would not be able to extend our life-span if we were not designed to live longer. Therefore, when we manage to control certain anomalies, such as disease, trauma, personality and behaviour flaws, drug addiction and self-destructive tendencies, the natural order of our existence prevails.

Since ancient times there have been people who, in an empirical or instinctive way, have adopted a lifestyle and thinking pattern which allowed them to reach a more advanced age while enjoying an excellent level of integral health. These are taken as examples by those who worship the past to assume, without any statistical basis, that our forebears were stronger and lived longer. They forget the millions of people who died in childbirth, at birth, or during childhood or prematurely due to eruptive fevers, whooping cough, tetanus, polio, rabies and so on.

These long-lived centenarians from the past are the same long-lived centenarians of today. People who have learnt the secret of living in mental and spiritual peace. They are individuals less concerned with social status and other people's expectations, than with the realisation of their own and very rational expectations. They are more identified with cooperation and service than with competition and eagerness for possessions and acquisition.

They are predominantly affable, happy, positive and loving people, not unfriendly, aggressive, hostile, grumbling individuals full of resentment. They are people capable of forgetting and overcoming adversity because they turn their eyes and thoughts away from their own adversity and direct their gaze towards other people's misfortune while never losing sight of the light of hope.

These people lived long lives before and are living long and healthy lives today. However, the reality is that most people in the past died before they reached fifty, whereas nowadays it is becoming more and more common to be over fifty still vigorous, energetic, interesting and attractive.

Admittedly a healthy longevity in the past was the privilege of just a few and is still only reached by a limited percentage of the world's population. However, without any doubt, the examples of healthy centenarians are now more visible and more frequent and everybody could be capable of reaching the three ciphers age.

How? By introducing a few changes in the way we focus our perception system and by adopting a healthy lifestyle. One that should include regular mental and physical activity accompanied with a happy carefree attitude. A healthy diet rich in vegetables and salads, low in fats specially in animals fats, plus a convenient supplementation of colloidal minerals, vitamins (especially Vitamin B 17 the anti-cancer vitamin), folic acid and anti-oxidants.

When reading the literal translation of an article on *The Aging Society*, which appeared in *Daedalus* magazine of The American Society of Arts and Science, written and compiled by Alan Pifer and Lydia Bronte of the Carnegie Foundation, its theme is that we are living through an historical moment in time, a moment where and when a new third age in life is not coming into existence, since it has always existed, but becoming sufficiently common as to be turning into a massive phenomenon.

Until recent times, only two ages stood as massive phenomena: youth and maturity. Youth was characterised by growth, learning and maturation; maturity involved productivity, reproduction and the care and guidance of the youth.

There have always been survivors above the sixty-five year barrier, though their cases were certainly not a majority. However, their number have been increasing since the turn of the twentieth century. By 1915 there were enough cases to prompt Prince Otto Von Bismarck, Chancellor of the German Empire, to propose a system of social security for these people who unexpectedly were surpassing the second age. Currently, many developed countries have readjusted their welfare systems to cover their age citizens, who are gradually becoming more numerous.

Dr Walter M Bortz, ex president of the American Geriatric Society, Associated Clinical Professor of the Faculty of Medicine in Stanford University with over 40 years experience, tell us that:

> 'We have recently inherited a new segment of life: The third age. This new phenomenon is raging over us, bringing in new decades of opportunities and something like the potential to profit from what used to be considered a waste. This phenomenon has caught us unprepared, due in part to the fact that the third age lacks a biological, psychological, sociological, economical and political definition. We have not encyclopaedias, textbooks, experiments or models for guiding us in our new age (English speaking nations and Europeans, in general, believe that what is new to them, must be new for the entire planet).
>
> The chances for conflict among people of different ages are real. Young people will not condescend to their elders simply because they're older; we must look for some kind of equity in the distribution of resources. We are not armed to face new challenges. We lack a conceptual frame in which to represent our new years and we are actually in the position of redefining our whole life.
>
> Our first challenge is to accept as natural a life-span of 120 years and to redefine its segments and sub-

segments. In the not distant future, youth will have to be considered as that segment of life stretching from birth to the age of 40, sub-divided into: juvenile youth (0-20) and adult youth (20-40). Middle age will be sub-divided into: early middle age (40-60) and late middle age (60-80). Third age will also be sub-divided into: early third age (80-100) and late third age (100-120). No one should die before late third age; any death before the age of 100 must be considered premature.

'The fact that the third age phenomenon is spreading, means that it is absolutely necessary to dedicate a great deal of responsible consideration to, not only the length of life the future has in store for us, but the quality of it. 'How much longer have we to live?' could be a question whose answer becomes numerically less important as the quality of the years ahead gain in prominence. *One minute of plenitude and happiness may be more acceptable than a few days of suffering.* Definitely though, a long life does not necessarily exclude it from being of good quality. On the contrary, a life of plenitude, happiness and exquisite quality increases the possibility of lengthening the number of years to be lived. Quality and quantity can and should be coherent one with the other'.

The famous biologist Stephen Gould stated:

'Big and small mammals are essentially similar. Their space and time in life depend on their life rhythm, and they all last approximately the same amount of biological time. Small mammals tic-tac very quickly, rapidly burning out, and thus live for a short time. Big mammals live longer at a slower pace. If measured by their own biological clock, mammals of different sizes tend to live the same length of time. All mammals regardless of their size, tend to breath two hundred millions times during their lives. Also their hearts beat around eight hundred million times. If measured according to their own biological clock in relation to the rate of their heartbeat and breathing, all mammals live approximately the same time.'

This statement by Stephen Gould illustrates the relative nature of time. Time is relative to the events it encloses and the frame within which it elapses. Time is an eminently subjective concept.

Could it be that in a world we imagine integrated and limited by the three dimensions known to us as length, width and depth that time could represent the fourth dimension? We're only lifting a corner of the veil that covers it all. We live in a world of mirages and physical phenomena that are just a façade of reality. The orchestra, the actors and the script of the play, together with its author, are still behind the scenes.

The truth is that our world is essentially mental-spiritual. The genuine time machine dreamt of by H.G. Wells is alive, pulsating and functioning within each of us. It is in our mind where choices are born. It is in our mind where we visualise our life-path. The real pilgrim is our own mind!

On the night prior to her assassination (not execution) on the guillotine by the revolutionaries of the time, the

Queen of France, Marie Antoinette's hair turned totally white. She had aged twenty or thirty years in the span of a few hours. The quality of life in her cell, during those few hours prior to her decapitation in all certainty was completely different to that she had previously experienced.

Going back to the topic of a biological clock, let's remember that overweight and unfit people have a much quicker heartbeat than those who are slim and fit. Very fit people have a very low heart rate (45-50 beats per minute). On the other hand obese people, smokers and those suffering hypertension have heart rates that exceed 70-80 beats per minute therefore burning out their machinery more rapidly.

Happy, positive, tolerant and satisfied people enjoy a peace of mind and spirit that translates into harmonious neuro-transmitters, hormones and neuro-receptors. This brings about an appropriate metabolic rate with balanced sleep and wakeful periods, a relaxed heartbeat, an optimal blood pressure and a gradual burning of calories, all of which helps add life to our years.

Competitiveness, aggressiveness and intolerance generates violent and negative emotions, which in turn provoke the discharge of catecholamines and adrenaline. These substances increase breathing and heart rates, blood pressure and rapid calorie loss, which consequently subtract years from our life, and life from our years.

The proven fact that artists, musicians, teachers and writers make up the longest-lived guilds is a good example of how creativity and continuous learning promote the state of mind and the blood chemistry conducive to a long and happy life.

In one way or another, the quality and the quantity of the years we live are a legacy of our consciousness, since we are gods playing at being naïve. A piece of life, or God's breathe dwells within us. This God inside us is the important one. A happy communication with this piece of life within us is the best medication.

COMMUNICATION

Woman, take my hand.
Let's walk together without rush,
Enjoying the wind its spirit and its breeze.
You'll learn to see the world
In a new way
And from the appropriate distance
To observe it all.
I'll teach you to live with the feeling
That simultaneously you are everywhere
And yet at no particular place.
Don't watch the clock, miss not the past.
Don't think the future is the desired fruit.
Limit yourself to enjoying what the present offers!
Allow not people opinions to alter your joy.
Open your mind to the heartbeat of the world
And climb the mountain of ecstasy.

Sergio Prado-Arnuero 1996

Human beings, like all other living creatures, use many means to communicate with their environment, with all other species, with their fellow man, with the society in which they live, with life (God) and with themselves. The word communication immediately brings to mind the use of the spoken and the written word, sign language and/or publicity advertisements with their stereotyped and subliminal images. Let's not forget that superior vertebrates have five senses: sight, hearing, taste, smell and touch. According to conventional anatomists and physiologist superior vertebrates receive almost all the information outside their bodies via these senses.

It is evident that all our changing inner states of mind and the multitude of ideas, thoughts, phobias, fixations, feelings and everything else related to our very rich inner life, are expressed by we superior vertebrates through vocal sounds, body movements (conscious or sub-conscious), gestures and attitudes. These become structured as a vocal or body code of language that is capable of translating, in a highly precise way, the contents of our thoughts.

We know our dog is happy and lovingly waiting for us because of the pricking of its ears, its eye expression, the continuous shifting of its entire body, but most specifically by the waging of its tail. We know the dog is scared when it hides its tail between its legs or when it become rigid with its fur erect in readiness to attack. To an expert a dog's breath provides information about its diet, for example, one and a half month old puppy's breath smells of milk. Cats express pleasure and acceptance by rubbing their fur against the legs of those it likes, and bristles when fearful or when feeling aggressive.

The skin of vertebrates also provides us with a huge amount of information; for example, when young the skin is silky, shiny and firm but becomes dull, wrinkled and saggy when old. Hair also provides information since it looses, its colour and may turn white/grey depending on a person's age or health. According to the predominance of wrinkles in different areas we can deduce if someone is chronically worried or if on the contrary smiles a lot simply because the pattern of wrinkling is different.

In humans, constant alcohol consumption causes chronic aging of the skin. It also gives to the sclerotic (the white part of the eyes) a slight yellowish/greenish tinge. In this way, guided by simple observation of the skin and eyes, we can reasonable guess who drinks heavily and who doesn't.

Just by shaking someone's hand we can gather a huge valuable amount of information. Is the skin rough? Is it soft? Is it warm, hot or cold? Is it sweaty, dry or clammy? Are the hand muscles firm? Is the hand bland and spongy, or hard and rigid? Is the hand fleshy or bony? Is the hand wide or slim? Are the fingers long or short? Is the owner trying to destroy our hand, are they friendly, competitive or aggressive or shy? Are they confident, insecure or overconfident?

How do you perceive its bone structure through the skin? Is it thin and brittle, or solid, thick and strong? Are the nails stained with nicotine? If your eyes were closed while shaking hands, would you be able to guess the other person's gender, race and some traits of his or her personality? Is it possible by just shaking hands, to have some insight into who has an open mind and who has a rigid and narrow criteria, who tends to accept changes easily and who is stubborn and fossilised in archaic concepts?

Nearly every day we shake a few hands, pat a few shoulders or have ours shoulders patted; we hug or are hugged, and we kiss or are kissed on the cheeks or other parts of our body. We sweat and our skin transpires odours that reveals information about our race, age, diet, habits and sometimes even about our social status. Our skin is a wonderful tool of communication which we use constantly either consciously or subconsciously. Logically then many communication problems will manifest themselves on the skin.

Fear makes us pale, while ire (anger) makes our skin red. Alcoholics try to disguise their fears, under the warmth of the drink the alcoholic looses fear and inhibitions and even boast of their outrage and aggressiveness. Their fearful and pale skin is also disguised, becoming red and warm. The following day, as they suffer the hangover, their heart races, alters its rate and produces occasional extra systoles (heartbeats). Once again their skin becomes pale, sweaty, cold and clammy while their hands may be hot, but also wet and sticky. Isn't this the picture of fear? Is there in every alcoholic a hidden depression loaded with fear? How many options does this underlying fear have to manifest itself? Is fear the reason why so many drinkers under the influence become strident, talkative, boastful and bullish?

Unlike fear, ire dyes us red. 'I was red with fury' is a phrase we often hear. Since we cannot wave our ire as a flag in society, we need to disguise it as 'irony' and you cannot be ironic on your own. Irony which is ire combined with wit, needs a social framework in order to reveal itself, and this social framework serves as a river bed either containing it or allowing it to flow. When this social frame is not at hand we are in desperate need of a cigarette. Smoking disguises a communication problem loaded with ire! In complying with its duty to disguise ire, smoking turns our skin

pale, therefore hiding the red skin colour that would reveal our inner state of mind.

At the root of any addiction such as alcoholism, smoking, drug addiction, workaholism, addiction to sex or any other human relationship there exists an addictive personality. An addictive personality is nothing but a form of manifestation of those giants of the soul—fear, ire and self-aversion (the opposite of self-esteem) and these giants of the soul find a way of expressing themselves on our skin.

I wonder up to what point is psoriasis, an unsightly scabbing of our skin, nothing else but a physical manifestation at skin level of a deep and perhaps hidden subconscious problem, a disguised aversion to socialisation? Could it be that it gives the psoriatic patient a shield with which to avoid social contact? Could the scabs reflect a, 'do not touch me, do not come too close to me' attitude?

Is adolescent acne screaming to us of the adolescent's inner fury? Isn't it a way of crying out for help to solve their lack of an inner sense of identity and belonging? Do they feel fragmented between the infancy they've just left behind and the adulthood they have not yet reached?

And what about the adolescent children of divorced parents, what level of fragmentation can they reach in such a situation? How much fury and frustration does this fragmentation provoke? Some express it openly but what about those who don't? Through which channel does this energy escape? Does it explode in a form of acne, denouncing an inner conflict and repression? Is not acne only the internalisation of this anger? What about the range of sexual and passionate impulses that emerge at this age to which they cannot give full rein? Does this conflict too result in an eruption on their skin?

Urine and excreta are also a form of communication and a source of information. They represent such an effective form of communication that dogs, wolves, tigers and other predators use their urine to mark territorial borders, to leave behind a track for orientation as an act of provocation or a threat to other animals. The worst insult or provocation a dog can offer another barking at him from the other side of the gate, while safely inside his own garden, is to cock his leg and urinate outside the gate.

Man copulates or makes love via an organ through which he, not only ejaculates, but urinates as well. The woman's vulva is both the vaginal introitus and the external orifice of her urethra. A sexual relationship that among other things, is also a very intense form of communication, brings into contact not only our reproductive organs, but also all the other organs of our five senses and the distal extremity of our urinary system.

During copulation we exchange breath, saliva and other bodily secretions, we fuse our bodies and energies syntonising in a grand communion of purpose, in an uninhibited desire to reach oneness, and total communication, and for a fleeting moment, during orgasm, we reach it. During orgasm we briefly return to 'paradise' and because this return is not permanent we are obsessed with repeating the experience as often as we can.

Everything written in this chapter on communication so far provides evidence that we use our skin, sweat, and urine and genital secretions to communicate. The air you breathe is the same air we all breathe. It is our atmosphere's way of establishing communication between us all. It is the planet's way of showing us the importance of our breath in the process of communication and it's way of forcing us to share the vital concern about environmental pollution. Some breaths are captivating while others are repellent.

Drunkards' breath is often described in police reports. In trains, buses, streets and social gatherings we can smell 'tobacco breath' before we've even seen the person responsible and for some time now police have been using a 'breathalyser' to measure the amount of alcohol circulating in our bloodstream via our breath. Amphetamines, cocaine and other stimulants of the central nervous system alter our breath in such a particular way that doctors, paramedics and nurses can recognise them immediately. Tranquillisers, diazepam's (Benzos) and barbiturates produce the same effect and can be detected in the same way. All of these drugs can also be detected in urine tests.

The breath, sweat, urine and faeces of carnivores usually give out smells much more unpleasant than those of vegetarians. Fear, among many other things, stimulates the secretion of catecholamines, adrenaline, nor-adrenaline, serotonins, and so on, altering the blood chemistry and all bodily odours. This is why we talk of 'the smell of fear'. Happy people have a more pleasant smell than those immersed in fear or ire.

Those of us who live surrounded by sports people are able to tell the difference between the smells in a boxing ring and those in a body building gymnasium. Groups of sports people, whether boxers, body builders, gymnasts, swimmers, track and field athletes, skaters, etc, have slightly different odours to the other groups.

When a sports person is close to extreme fatigue their muscles become loaded with lactic acid and their oxygenation capacity decreases dramatically. This is due to a saturation of lactic acid and an excessive increase in the demand for oxygen. Even if this person won't confess his or her exhaustion, or what is a worse try to hide it, they would not be able to because of the purplish tinge of the lips and skin, the smell of their breath and sweat which reveals their state of acidosis. This is simple non-verbal communication—body language!

Diabetics, depending on their sugar levels at a particular time, may produce an acidotic breath or an apple smelling breath. Why do insects bite some people more often than others? The country folk of Nicaragua explain this particular preference of mosquitoes by stating 'it is because you have sweet blood! They are not stating that the victim is diabetic, they are telling only that the victim has some sweet traits of personality that manifest in some smell preferred by mosquitoes (inter-species communication).

Modern conventional medicine uses a great deal of laboratory tests as auxiliary methods of diagnosis. The breathalyser or breath test to measure alcohol levels;

gasometry for asthma, bronchitis and other types of breathing deficiencies; haematic biometrics and blood chemistry for a long list of diseases. There are also tests involving saliva (sputum), urine, sweat, vaginal, urethral, throat and ear secretions.

The laboratories conducting these tests are establishing an intimate form of communication with the patient via their breath, sweat, urine and other secretions and excretions? Which stretch of the evolutionary path saw man loose the capacity to interpret the messages in theirs and others sweat, skin, urine, digestive system, central nervous system signals and all the other secretions and excretions?

It appears there are dogs capable of diagnosing prostate cancer just by sniffing the urine of the patient. Is this phenomenon something incredible? Of course not! Many clinicians from the developing countries have been doing this for some time. There are times in which we are able to smell death in a patient some weeks before it actually happens.

The skin, respiratory tract, urinary tract and reproductive system are all tools of communication. Through these tools we can present to the outside world, not only the problems of our organic functions, but also our emotional states and the particular features of our thought processes.

Infections, inflammations and complaints of the skin (acne, psoriasis, vitiligo, spots, etcetera), of the respiratory tract (asthma, tonsillitis, bronchitis, bronchiectases, etc), of the urinary tract (cystitis, pyelonephritis, renal deficiency etcetera), of the reproductive system (orchitis-swelling of the testicles, salpingitis-swelling of the fallopian tubes and ligaments etcetera) are manifestations of an underlying problem of communication that we are avoiding to face or that which we are dealing with in the wrong way.

Alcoholism, smoking, drug addiction, dependency, co-dependency, workaholism (addiction to work) are all telling us the same thing. Fear is behind all of them. We live in a society that has made an entire eulogy of fear. Terrorism exists only because fear dwells within each one of us turning us into a political, economic or religious terrorist. The rejection of our fellowmen is so often disguised as morality...moral terrorism?

Disease will be overcome when we can replace fear with love and when we learn to communicate in the same way that we vibrate within this beautiful emotion. Then, the legacy of our consciousness will be altered for the best and we will realise that we are gods playing at being naive.

> Woman, take my hand
> And entwine your fingers with mine.
> Let's walk together without rush, anguish or fear,
> Enjoying the wind, its spirit and its breeze.

CO-DEPENDENCY

I begin this chapter with two quotes from the Chinese book *The I Ching*, translated and interpreted by Richard Wilhelm. In a section of the hexagram No 61 called *The Inner Truth*, talking about the third line the book states:

'The root of all influx lies within the inner self. If his centre of gravity lies in others, no matter how close to them we may be, we are inevitably tossed to and fro between joy and sorrow. Rejoicing to high heaven, then sad onto death.

'This is the fate of those who depend upon an inner accord with other persons whom they love. Here we have only the statement of the law that this is so. Whether this condition is felt to be an affliction or the supreme happiness of love, is left to the subjective verdict of the person concerned.'

This chapter looks into the characteristics in forming a type of personality that is present in all of us to a greater or lesser degree. This personality type plays mean tricks on us and among other things leads us to suffer a physical malaise sometimes labelled as an illness. I am referring to the addictive personality. When talking about this personality we are forced to analyse the process of dependency and co-dependency that integrates at the main level of its manifestation.

This personality type manifests itself via various sub-syndromes, all responding to the same basic structure such as: alcoholism, smoking, drug addiction, workaholism, bulimia (an exaggerated uncontrollable appetite), anorexia nervosa, sexual promiscuity as well as an exaggerated attachment to love relationships and co-dependency. In order to deal effectively with these sub-syndromes we must bear in mind that they all respond to the same addictive process. Therefore, we must treat the symptoms of the sub-syndrome while, at the same time, supporting the process of overcoming the basic addictive personality.

At the core of human and family relationship problems we frequently find an addictive personality. Into the welfare field, especially concerning alcohol and drugs, or as a family relationship counsellor, or as a mental health worker it is impossible to successfully address any issue without keeping in mind the disruptive role of the addictive personality. Without treating this disorder of our consciousness we cannot permanently solve any problem.

Co-dependency is a disorder of our consciousness increasingly present in our daily relationships. Our society promotes a fake sense of independence from our parents and educators, while stimulating a system of validation based on external frames of reference. Societal recognition is a perceived vital element to the health of our self-esteem. We feel that our self, in order to be strong, has to have public recognition.

There are many books and articles written about the highest risk groups of co-dependency. Here is a list by Sharon Weismeider Cruse, a renowned specialist on this subject:

- The wives of addicts or recovering addicts.
- The adult children of alcoholics
- The children, grandchildren and siblings of workaholics
- Professionals who work with addicts
- Families with a trauma or a hidden secret
- Families that do not encourage autonomy
- Families that reward weakness and hopeleness
- As well as those who live with someone who is neurotic.

The core of co-dependency rests on the very promoted and widely advertised tendency of self-validation using almost exclusively, external frames of reference. The tendency of emphasising goals rather than the journey, of branding quality according to degrees of acceptance, of equalising quality with the capacity to produce financial benefits and of evaluating others for what they have, or achieve, is at the core of the addictive personality.

Individuals establish relationships with substances, people and activities according to a pattern which is determined by their personality type. Those with an addictive personality relate to other people in the same way they might with alcohol or another drug. They become pathologically attached to the other person and will do anything to keep the relationship going. They do not allow the establishment of well-defined borders. They cannot live without the other and their social as well as their emotional security depends of the relationship.

Poets and singers promote and praise this kind of relationship and society takes on the job of training us to look for and to idealise it. That is why the most disturbing tragedies are taking place daily in this type of relationship; a relationship that our culture has taught us to mystify. We are brought up and conditioned to place our centre of gravity outside ourselves.

> 'The root of all influx lies within the inner self. If his centre of gravity lies in others, no matter how close to them we may be, we are inevitably tossed to and fro between joy and sorrow.'
>
> *The I Ching*

Materialistic scientists with their lineal logic (cause-effect) teach us to look for causes that are palpable, probable and can be recreated outside of ourselves! Thank God for the existence of what is called 'the margin of autonomy' which is made up of people who, in spite of all the efforts to condition members of a given society (be it a consumer of a free market society, a totalitarian society—a centralised and almost always poorly planned economy), stick to their convictions by maintaining, in a conscious or sub-conscious way, a perennial inner dialogue with their 'Superior I', their Divine root, their inner Self...Life itself.

Co-dependency is a problem of the consciousness. Education, culture and biology are extremely important conditions or factors, but the essence of the disorder still resides in the consciousness. Co-dependency is a problem of communication with our 'Father' and even if we see it as a social problem it is a problem of 'social consciousness!' stemming from a lack of communication of an entire society with our life itself.

Co-dependents have no idea where they end and others begin. This is so because they have lost sight of the fact that their body is only the temple where the 'Holy Trinity' dwells. They have lost sight of the fact that we, being just a microscopic part of the Whole, are in ourselves a Whole. We are a complete, unique, surprisingly beautiful, complex and marvellous universe within ourselves.

A co-dependant person is fragmented and none of their fragments exercises any authority over the rest because this authority has been placed outside the self. Authority has been placed on a substance such as alcohol, tobacco or drugs; on their job; on an activity or a person; or maybe on a particular church or religion; a political party or some other organisation; on fashion or the latest stereotypes dictated by mass media, glamour magazines or Hollywood.

J. Krishnamurti, when speaking on individuality states:

> 'The word "individuality" means indivisible, not fragmented. Individuality involves stability, the whole, and the word whole means Healthy, Sacred. But you are not an individual, you are not healthy because you are shattered into pieces, fractioned within yourself, you are in contradiction with yourself, separated, and therefore you are not an individual at all. And within this fragmentation, how can you expect one of the fragments to assume authority over the other fragments?'

Co-dependents become a mirror of the emotions; they lack borders; they become confused when others are confused, depressed when the atmosphere around them is depressive, furious or happy when others display these emotions. This is mass psychology as masses are co-dependant. All changes within the co-dependant come from outside and there is no inner conductor, there are no borders the co-dependant takes from others sadness, happiness, fear or anything else that those around are feeling or thinking.

We have been trained by our family, the educational system and the church to be dependant, to value ourselves using an external frame of reference or social framework invested with features that are supposedly more important than our own values and convictions. They teach us to think what we are told to think, feel what we are told to feel, see what we are told to see, and above all, know what they want us to know. I call this 'cultural training in co-dependency', there is also in society a 'cultural training in violence'.

We learn that the points of reference for our thoughts, feelings, knowledge and values are external to the self. As a result of this we become borderless people. In order to have and experienced borders, the person must begin by adopting internal points of reference by getting to know his/her thoughts and feelings from the inside and to have a clear idea of his/her own authentic priorities. From these internal points of reference they will be able to relate with their surroundings, departing from the perspective of a very strong and assertive self.

Now we can understand why co-dependents have such difficulty in having warm, intimate relationships. They escape from these relationships and from their house to their club, to the 'pub', to church, to their business appointments or else they plunge into frantic housework escaping from the opportunities to become intimate or genuinely tender and loving with what and who life offers them. This is because in order to be intimate, one needs a strong and genuine sense of self. If there is no sense of self, every time there is intimacy between two people they finish fused, confused and blended into the life of the other. They loose their individuality. Therefore the co-dependant in order to survive escapes from intimacy.

Poets also add their bit to encourage co-dependency. To highlight this look at the poem *Nocturno a Rosario* by Manuel Acuña.

> And so…I need to tell you that I love you,
> Tell you that I adore you with all my heart
> That I suffer so much that I cry so much
> That I cannot bear any longer
> And I cry out, imploring and speaking
> On behalf of my last illusion
> I want you to know
> That for many days now
> I have felt ill and wane
> From so much lack of sleep
> All my hopes have died away
> And my nights are dark
> So dark and sombre
> That I can't even see
> Where my future lies hidden.

Elsewhere, the same poem states:
> I understand your lips will never be mine.
> I understand your eyes will never, ever, see me.

Yet I love you!
And in my crazy and fiery ravings I adore...your
　disdain,
I forgive your indifference
And instead of loving you less, I love you even
　more.

This poem is a clear example of what is mistakenly called romantic love. Truly it is dependant love as romanticism and dependency are closely related. It may well be the reason why its author committed suicide the very night he wrote it.

A lack of borders is easily observed in families of alcoholics. In such a family each member lives the alcoholic's problem, and the alcoholic himself enjoys the situation. Up to a certain point, the family's preoccupation nurtures his/her alcoholism. Family life in its entirety revolves around this person, and he/she enjoys being the centre of attention. The family grants the alcoholic the power to define them and to determine their states of mind and their actions and reactions.

As the illness progresses the borders within the family unit become less defined and the fusion of all its members becomes more intense. If one of them decides to step out of this vicious circle and learn to be themselves, they are seen as a family deserter. Emotional blackmail, in the form of sentimental rebukes and moral arguments will follow.

Co-dependents are forever trying to project the image of 'a good person'. This is not objectionable in itself. What makes this feature pathological is the exaggerated importance that reaching this objective has for them. They are complacent and have developed amazing skills in finding out what people like and dislike. They truly believe that if they adjust themselves to what other people want they will be safe and accepted. They are forever seeking attention and acceptance. They are slaves of 'grandeur expectations' that they deposit on their own and their beloved shoulders. Simultaneously they think in terms of success or failure so when the irrational expectations cannot be met they consider themselves, and their loved ones, as failures.

They don't trust their own perceptions and resort to seeking external validation, to them the opinion of a social framework is vital. Co-dependents doubt that anyone can love them for their intrinsic value, so they try to become indispensable. We all know friends that insist on doing us a 'favour', one we never asked for, and pressure us to accept it. They are always 'doing for others'. Co-dependents have a strong need to be needed.

Co-dependents are eternal martyrs. They suffer and do it with dignity, gallantly believing they do it for a holy cause when in reality they are only trying to perpetuate a destructive situation and keeping others away from the possibility of becoming themselves. These martyrs maintain chaotic situations spoiling alcoholics and addicted people without allowing them to face their problem and their sad reality. Their actions appear to be so gallant that it becomes very difficult to see them as a symptom of a spiritual disease. Physical ailments affect co-dependents as an external manifestation of their spiritual disease. They develop headaches, backaches, lung and heart diseases as well as gastro-intestinal disorders. Appetite disorders, such as bulimia and anorexia nervosa, have their roots deeply implanted in co-dependency. In the unchaining of extreme cases during adolescence we find an almost absolute lack of intrinsic self-esteem. This lack creates an excessive desire to respond to the physical stereotypes imposed by fashion. Many Hollywood and socialite celebrities could be a great example.

The predominantly superficial and peripheral communication of our individual conscience, with the social conscience enveloping us, is what triggers all those diseases which have their roots in our emotional world. Endeavouring always to respond to the expectations of the outside world frustrates, frightens and compels us to live immersed in the world of outward appearances. A consciousness forced to walk in tight shoes is a lame consciousness! A consciousness dressed in extremely tight clothes is a consciousness that cannot breath properly resulting in a disorder of the respiratory system.

A consciousness forever covered from head to toe will never receive the sunlight or ventilate itself resulting in a disorder of the skin. The skin becomes covered in fungus; it is itself a fungus! A consciousness plagued with all these problems needs to constantly try on different shoes, but most often their priority is style and not comfort so the problem remains. This consciousness needs to change its clothes and wrappings, if these changes are always dictated by the demands of outward appearances the problem continues and becomes complicated with compulsive consumerism.

In the case of dependency, just as with any other pathological disorder, the problem lays not so much in the social structures as on the type of communication we establish between our individual consciousness and the predominant social consciousness.

Are not individuals responsible for pioneering a new and more sensitive social consciousness? It's very comfortable to be part of the herd and later take joy in blaming the system but we are part of the system, we live from and within the system, therefore, we *are* the system.

TOBACCOISM

'Continue to contaminate your own bed, and one night you will suffocate in your own waste.'

Chief Seattle.

The compulsive consumption of tobacco is a strongly addictive habit that has fatal consequences to the individual, those close to them, and to the community as a whole. Around the time of the second world war and the years following, smoking was considered 'chic' due partly to the stereotyped images of popular movie stars. Images such as Marlene Dietrich with her seductive sleepy eyes and her skirt slit up to her thighs inhaling smoke via a long cigarette holder inspired at least three generations of western civilised people.

First through the cinema, and later via television, Hollywood has promoted this over-acted cliché in light of the latest natural trends. Hollywood created a ridiculous stereotype of a very confident, seductive and experienced man who while having a sardonic and challenging smile on his face had a cigarette peevishly hanging from the corner of his mouth.

Cigarette companies exploited this cliché and popularised commercials in which the same stereotype appeared dressed as a cowboy riding a horse while performing 'virile chores'. The Marlboro Man, and consequently those—like me—who saw themselves as virile smoked Marlboro. The Marlboro Man stereotype sometimes swaps his horse for a motorcycle or a sports car and his cowboy clothes for formal attire but his style of smoking and overall attitude is still very much the same. The world embraced approvingly the likes of Butch Cassidy, the Sundance Kid, Bonnie and Clyde, Clint Eastwood, James Dean and Marlon Brandon all who incarnated a variant of the Marlboro Man.

And so in a subliminal and marvellously concealed way several generations have been led to avoid analysing their own insecurities and to place all their communication problems in the trenches behind a weapon of self-defence. A weapon capable of burning the skin with its sparks and provoking tears, coughing and choking attacks with the smoke it releases—the cigarette!

What a wonderful trick of camouflage. The emotionally weaker you are, the more you will project an image of an offensive challenge chewing on a pretended cartridge of dynamite that 'per se' introduces you into 'The Marlboro World'. Later in commercials the mass media introduced a very attractive woman staring in admiration at these inveterate smokers...bingo!...danger, power, adventure and instant sex appeared to be in just one single packet of cigarettes!

In order of widening the spectrum of the tobacco market, Hollywood now includes financial and professional successful people performing ordinary task while smoking. They now are trying to make us associate smoking with relaxing processes in stressful times.

It was in this way that the horrifying and diabolic dance of 'the billions' commenced, a dance that revolves around tobacco and its rhythmical and seductive beat. A dance which has enveloped statesmen, doctors, owners and participants of enterprises, housewives and the ordinary man in the street. A dance that hushes the conscience and hides the truth. How often have I heard someone expressing concern and pity for those caught in drug addiction, while calmly smoking one cigarette after another. These people believe drug addiction has nothing to do with them, that all they do is smoke cigarettes, something even a priest might do.

This wave of drug abuse around the globe is becoming gigantic and uncontrollable. It is growing as a consequence of corruption and lack of scrupulous manufacturers and dealers. It is growing as a consequence of financial and political colonialism exercised by the industrialised and well-developed countries upon the developing countries and at an individual level as a consequence of unfulfilled expectations planted in our minds by family, teachers and the society in which we live. Expectations that breed addictive personalities as they try to fit into the accepted stereotypes promoted by society. The mystification of hard work as a presentation card that proves you are a citizen of the highest quality. The mystification of success, sexual liberation (frequently understood as promiscuity), efficiency, aggressiveness and violence (often disguised as determination) generates frustration and feelings of inadequacy in those who feel they cannot be the 'winners' their families expect them to be.

Millions of young people live in a world where they feel they don't belong and want to escape to a reality of their own. They feel they lack an outlet which gives them a sense of self-worth and self-esteem, so they choose the ingestion, injection or inhalation of a drug to carry them far away from their painful reality, or at least from their painful perception of their own reality. Fortunately, a considerable number of our youth are becoming day by day more alert and informed about the very concept of addiction. They are more aware each day of the adverse effects of addictive substances acting upon addictive personalities. They are more interested in problems such as environmental pollution and social justice. Slowly they are consolidating the notion that the problem of addiction lies within the unjust social structures; the lack of individual awareness and the prevalence of double standards.

Families are social units which reflect the predominant culture of the society as a whole. Within their families, young people see their parents smoking like chimneys and drinking coffee like wartime pilots. They smell their uncle, who reeks of alcohol every day of the year, constantly criticise their use of marijuana. On television they see supposedly successful people opening their refrigerator getting a beer each time they arrive at home. How can we prevent them from falling into some kind of addiction when we are setting these examples? What moral stature do we have to criticise addicts to illicit drugs? Cigarettes are the major killers in the world. The main preventable cause of premature death on this planet is tobacco!

Nicotine is the best known ingredient in tobacco, albeit only one of the four thousands ingredients resulting from the combustion of cigarettes. The toxins derived from long periods of smoking are related to multiple chemical compounds, each and every one of them harmful to the health. The one that stimulates dependency and addiction is nicotine.

Nicotine is present in cigarette smoke and in the tiniest particles which are rapidly absorbed and deposited in the bloodstream at lung level. Most cigarettes contain between 0.5 and 2.0 milligrams of nicotine depending on the brand. Like the majority of psychoactive drugs, nicotine is also rapidly distributed. It penetrates the brain crossing the meningeal barrier. It is capable also of crossing the placental barrier and shows up in all body fluids including breast milk. A breast-fed baby can have nicotine blood levels as high as the mothers. Approximately 80-90% of the nicotine absorbed by the active or passive smoker, is metabolised in the liver before being excreted in the urine, sweat, saliva, milk, etcetra.

Nicotine exercises powerful effects on the brain, spinal cord, peripheral nervous system, heart, cardio-vascular system and other structures of our body. Inside our nerves cells, or through their influence on our glands, all drugs and known poisons are fabricated.

A synapse, the connection between one nerve cell with another for the purpose of transmitting sensations, impulses or messages is not a physical connection. The nerve end of one cell is slightly separated from the nerve end of its neighbouring cell. The impulse or message does not jump from one cell to the other. Each cell in order to communicate with the other secretes a chemical substance called a neuro transmitter. For each neuro transmitter sent carrying its coded message there is a specific neuro receptor (another chemical substance) on the receiving cell to decode this message. If we lack these specific neuro receptors drugs and poisons are powerless to act within our bodies.

External drugs and poisons, substances not fabricated within our body, mimic our neuro transmitters and trick the specific neuro receptors in charge into receiving them as messengers. Therefore they displace the organic substances, due to the chemical similarity between the external drug and our neuro transmitters.

We fabricate a type of neuro transmitter called endorphin, a substance that has an analgesic and euphoric producing function, morphine produced in pharmacological laboratories displaces our own endorphin and saturates the nerve cell's neuro receptors. Externally produced morphine is never as pure and adequate as the substance fabricated by our body. If we start to saturate ourselves with artificially fabricated drugs, the cells in charge of producing their own become sluggish in their function and later, when the pharmacological substance is not available we'll experience a deficiency in this specific neuro transmitter (withdrawal syndrome). This works in such a way that if a street fabricated drug does not find a specific neuro receptor to receive it, it will not have an effect on us. This specific neuro receptor only exists where our bodies are fabricating the specific neuro transmitter that matches it. Any drug capable of influencing us does so because we also manufacture it in our body. In this way alcohol affect us because we produce from sugar a minimal amount of alcohol in our system. Marijuana affects us because we produce a twin chemical substance called anandamide, a catecholamine with tranquillising and moderately euphoria producing effects. Tobacco affects us because we fabricate a substance called nicotinamide, a very close chemical relative to nicotine but with beneficial effects. This rule applied to any psychoactive drug.

Nicotine mimics, copies and imitates nicotinamide displacing it and deceiving the neuro-receptors that receive it. It also deceives the receptors of another substance called acetylcholine. This is manifested as a stimulus to the central nervous system bringing about a rise in blood pressure and heart rate. Also, it encourages the release of epinephrine, known as adrenaline, by the suprarenal glands that produces symptoms characteristic of a fight/fright/flight response.

Like any other stimulant drug nicotine has a rebound effect and a period of depression following a fall in blood pressure. Nicotine also stimulates the tone and activity of the intestinal tract and bladder causing many to head for the bathroom after a smoke. Nicotine causes nausea and vomiting due to the stimulation of both the brain centre for vomiting (located at the brain stem), and the receptors of the gastric mucosa, but a tolerance to this effect rapidly develops. This drug is also capable of inducing a slight shaking of the hands. In large doses it can trigger convulsions, epileptics therefore, have even more reason to avoid smoking. Nicotine stimulates the hypothalamus to release an antidiuretic hormone (ADH) resulting in retention of fluids. Further, it slows down the activity of the afferent nerves, which go from the muscles to the brain or the spinal cord, leading to a reduction in muscle tone. Therefore, those who wish to keep a slim and firm body image should avoid smoking.

In arteries of the heart afflicted with arteriosclerosis, as in the case of patients suffering from angina pectoris, high blood pressure or diabetes nicotine can cause ischaemia. Ischaemia is a deficiency in the oxygenation of any tissue. In the case of heart tissue it occurs through a doubled-barrelled mechanism. Firstly, it provokes vaso-constriction that decreases the amount of blood, and subsequently oxygen, which reaches any body tissue. Secondly, as it accelerates the heart rate it increases the hearts demand for blood and oxygen at precisely the time in which the cardio-vascular system, due to the constriction of the vessels, is rendered inefficient to respond to an increase in demand. This can precipitate a heart attack–myocardial infarction.

Nicotine induces physiological and psychological dependency, and is the most widely publicised example of drug dependency in statistics in the United States. The conclusions reached after a thorough study on tobacco addiction point out that:

a) Cigarettes and other types of tobacco are harmful.
b) Nicotine is the drug contained in tobacco that causes addiction.
c) The pharmacological processes and the behaviour determining tobacco addiction are similar to those which determine the addiction to other drugs, such as heroine and cocaine

d) More than 30,000 addicts in the United States die every year as a result of their tobacco addiction (this figure is steadily increasing each year).

Nicotine is slightly weaker than amphetamines or cocaine in reinforcing behaviour, but it limits the ability of the smoker to stop and think. To continue smoking is not just a question of free choice or habit. Smoking is a genuine addiction, which usually brings about adverse results to one's health.

In the case of tobacco, the abstinence or withdrawal syndrome (widely printed in many text books and pamphlets), is characterised by a desperate desire for nicotine, resulting in irritability, anxiety, anger, difficulty with concentration, sleeplessness, hunger and impatience. The syndrome lasts approximately a month, a fact proven by so many relapses in people who had successfully overcome the initial stages of withdrawal.

Could perhaps the withdrawal syndrome bring out into the open those personality traits that were hidden under the effects of the nicotine? If we squeeze an orange, it will give us orange juice, no force could make it give us grape or apple juice. In the same way, the abrupt withdrawal of a drug and the symptoms caused by its withdrawal can bring forth traits that were hidden, but not traits that were non-existent!

An effective treatment of tobacco addiction is difficult, since its causes are not clearly identified. Many place the blame on the addictiveness of nicotine, others place it on the mass media because of its alienating and conditioning effects. Doctors and physiologists believe they found the key to its cause in studies of neuro-transmitters and neuro-receptors.

Tobacco is simply a way out, an escape valve from inner pressures. Nicotine is not the problem—the problem is within us. Nicotine is only a way of disguising the problem. Without it smokers would show themselves as they really are cranky, impatient, aggressive, competitive and chauvinist (even in the case of a woman). A cigarette allows them to socialise, laugh and be tolerant. The day when they will overcome their tobacco addiction will be the day when they are capable of happiness, understanding and intimacy without the use of nicotine.

No matter how long it is since their last cigarette and how much protection and emotional support we offer, if the smoker does not strengthen their own inner centre of gravity, they will fall again into the habit at the slightest crisis.

Suppressing the nicotine without first tending to one's basic system of perception, thoughts and emotions does not work! It is not a case of will power. The will, like any other force or power, is exercised against a certain resistance and this is simply violence. The cigarette is precisely fulfilling its role of hiding violence and producing some chemical changes allowing the smoker to co-exist in peace. The secret lies in causing these changes by altering the existing system of perception and values.

Anger and fear can be marvellously camouflaged behind the curtain of tobacco smoke or behind the stereotyped images of 'the Marlboro Man/Woman'.

Smokers would be wise to look inside themselves for the root of their fears and insecurities. Within ourselves lie all communication and addiction problems. Disguises and make-up do not solve the conflict, although I must admit, they do hide it, soften it and make it more bearable. To take the cigarette away from someone who has not yet changed their way of thinking is sheer torture.

To socialise with oneself is every human's first duty. A smoker is someone who has lost the ability to socialise even with themselves without a cigarette. It is impossible to have an adequate external framework for socialising if there is no adequate internal framework.

Tobacco addiction is a problem of self-communication. The first step, as always, is to teach the smoker how to find and utilise their own inner resources, and to discover through internalising, meditation, visualisation and prayer the legacy of their own consciousness. There will be a very pleasant surprise waiting, for after all: we are all Gods, playing at being naïve.

MENOPAUSE

'Change is not without inconvenience, even from
worse to better.'

Samuel Johnson

This is a phase of spiritual individual evolution we
must happily accept and endeavour to fulfil with
merriment, so as to learn to enjoy that part of life in
which we initiate our return trip to oneness. This return
trip to oneness must necessarily undergo a
reconciliation of opposites within us. This individual
evolution may become a collective step forward if the
great majority of people in a given society have
managed to reconcile the opposites within themselves.

I would like to clarify that I have chosen the term
'reconciliation' of the opposites instead of 'fusion or
merging' because in this process the opposites don't
disappear, they coexist in a harmonious and
complementary way. It is possible to reconcile the
elements of both sexes which coexist within us, and at
the same time, keep our sexual identity intact, without
necessarily becoming bi or homosexual.

Marriage as a human institution is a good attempt,
occasionally effective, to stimulate the reconciliation of
opposites outside ourselves. Marriage is used as an
instrument of promoting communion of common
economic and social goals as a socially acceptable
channel to mutual physical/sexual attraction and to
create within the family unit the structure as defined by
the society in which we live.

The fact that only a very small percentage of couples marry for love has caused this conciliatory process to fail. Most people marry because of intense physical attraction, social-economic convenience, social pressure, fear of loneliness, to escape parental authority or by parental imposition. Very few couples in reality marry for love or inner affinity. Many will argue that although marriage is failing it satisfactorily fulfils its social role when needed and still has much to give to humanity. I agree with them. Actually, the family structure resulting from marriage is a faithful representation of a particular state of consciousness evolution, mutually mirrored with the social structure. An authentic and loving reconciliation of opposites has to take place within the human soul first. It is a prerequisite for achieving a genuine reconciliation inside marriage and consequently also within the entire society.

If it is true that the institution of marriage worked for the economic convenience of the patriarchal social system, it is also true that in most cases it was supported by a moral double standard full of lies and hypocrisy resulting in a high cost of suffering and renunciation to the wife.

Opposites never can be reconciled as a result of the labour of marriage. The institution of marriage will be more genuine, joyful and loving, reflecting an authentic reconciliation of opposites, when this reconciliation process has already occurred within the human soul. Then, and only then, will the true role of matrimony begin to reveal itself.

If men despise and loath the feminine element that exist within them, how can they love their wives, mothers, sisters, daughters, female friends, female workmates or female boss? Male chauvinism (machismo) is a spiritual illness based on rejection and fear of the feminine side of male personality. They live attached and in love with their virility. Could be this a huge homosexual narcissism?

Now then, what about feminism! Isn't it the same? Isn't it perhaps identification with 'male rights' and an attempt to acquire them? Isn't it a 'move over,' I'll step 'in scenario'? Doesn't it then, originate in an ambivalent rejection and hatred of one side of their being, which later, is projected outwards as rejection and hatred of men in general? In what way is a feminist any better than a male chauvinist?

In both cases the person is spiritually lacking. They are both immersed in polarity, which is a very dualistic view of the world. Both are totally fossilised on the obsolete, and crystallised on the past, refusing to grow. Both have lost their way in their return to paradise and oneness, to the reconciliation of the opposites. Both, the male chauvinist and the feminist, are incapable of authentic and tender intimacy since both are incapable of establishing relationships based on love, understanding, tolerance and tenderness. Their relationships are highly competitive and turbulent as both are prone to arm wrestling with their partner and to living in love with 'power'.

The failure of marriage as the ideal way of reconciling the opposites is only a temporary failure. It is a crisis, which is destined to be overcome. Out of this crisis, marriage will emerge changed, even improved. It will cease to be a disguise at reconciliation and instead will become the external projection of an authentic reconciliation of opposites hopefully taking place firstly within the human soul.

This lack of love and acceptance of that side which represents the opposite gender within us produces premature impotence in men. In women, along with other things, the lack of reconciliation of the opposites causes premenstrual syndrome and menopause with a display of climacteric symptoms. In both sexes it produces arterial hypertension, cholesterol problems, type A personality, and a long list of problems in affective sexual relationships.

At the beginning of this chapter I said that menopause is a phase of spiritual, individual and collective evolution. However, according to the *Collins Medical Dictionary* menopause is the final reproductive stage in women when the ovaries cease producing Graf follicles (in charge of ovulation) and therefore, the cessation of menstrual bleeding.

Menopause usually occurs between forty and fifty-four years of age. At this point the production of oestrogen hormone is low. The influence of these hormones prevail in the formation of secondary sexual features such as breasts, rounded hips, the feminine voice etcetera, features that wielded our mother Eve such formidable influence over our father Adam. Simultaneously there exists a decrease in the production of progesterone and this seems to be responsible for an accelerated loss of calcium, resulting in lighter, thinner, fragile and more brittle bones—a condition known as osteoporosis.

The reduction in the levels of oestrogen seems to be responsible for vaginal atrophy, a process leading to the loss of elasticity and narrowing of the vagina which adopts the shape of a semi-rigid and cardboard-like funnel. Additionally, the epithelium (mucosa covering the inner walls of the vagina) thins and dries and the vagina loses its capacity to self-lubricate and transmit that specific and pleasurable feeling it used to transmit during intercourse. Women, at least at this local level, lose their ability to provide their partner with the same pleasure they used to provide. Even sometimes the sexual act may become unpleasant and painful (dyspareunia).

The different physical symptoms, especially the vasomotor, mental and emotional symptoms we usually associate with menopause belong to what doctors call the 'climacteric syndrome'. Probably the name is derived from 'climate' and is associated with the hot flushes so notorious with this syndrome.

During menopause a gradual, progressive reduction in the function of the ovaries occurs as well as a variety of endocrine, somatic and psychological changes. As life expectancies are increasing for women, especially in the first world, women now spend a third of their lives in post menopause, a time when there is an absence of reproductive function.

In the last months preceding the onset of menopause the last menstrual cycles become irregular as does the duration and amount of bleeding. In the majority of cases the duration of the menstrual bleeding gradually shortens, until it stops altogether.

The objective symptoms, those changes objectively detectable in the female anatomy, are accompanied by subjective symptoms. By the former I refer to a reduction in the size and turgescence of the breast, narrowing and loss of elasticity of the vagina, along with atrophy of the vaginal and urogenital mucosa, as well as a speeding up of the process of osteoporosis. By the latter, or subjective symptoms, I refer to vasomotor instability, hot flushes, profuse sweating (specially at night), nervousness, anxiety, irritability and depression.

Any person in an embarrassing situation presents with vasomotor symptoms and blushes. 'I was red with embarrassment and my face was so hot', is what we often hear when people describe how they felt in this situation. Regardless of age or sex whenever we feel embarrassed we sweat, we become nervous, anxious, irritable and even depressed. Isn't it the same for menopause? The loss of that which we link to our sexual identity, our sexual polarity, depresses and embarrasses us. Therefore, at a somatic level, doesn't a chronic syndrome of embarrassment settle in as an external reflection of a singular state of consciousness? A consciousness characterised by a rejection of the return path to unity, generated by an excessive fondness for this sexual polarity?

No situation is bad if we know how to adjust to it. In the origin of our sufferings we always find a lack of 'acceptance'. We grow up when we learn to say 'Amen'…let it be so. We learn to be happy when exercise a joyful acceptance of life as it is…meaning the Divine Will. Then we become in tune with time, we adjust to the laws of time and space and are happy with our destiny, without wasting energies in sham resistance. The inviolability of the law of movement, which follows the path of lesser resistance, is applicable even in the emotional field. 'Natural laws are not external to things, but the harmony of the immanent movement within everything.' (I Ching Hexagram No 16 *Enthusiasm*).

For many years, within the body of women, the ovaries have been secreting hormones to help them to live, to develop and to unfold in this polarised world that rejects ambiguity, that compulsively seeks defined concepts and likes to establish separatist boundaries between countries, race, religion, colours, ethnicities, gender and priorities.

Those with a highly polarised way of thinking forget that any position of an object varies in relation to the position from which we observe it. Starting from the premise that they are the 'axis of the universe' they consider and express it categorically, that everything situated at their right belongs to the right side of the cosmos no matter where it happens to be placed. It is applicable to individuals as well as to nations. This is why they hoist and wave separatist concepts of right and left, evolution and creation, capitalism and socialism, chauvinism and feminism, good and evil, heterosexual and homosexual, life and death. But we come from oneness. We are an infinite particle of the Great and Colossal Cosmic Conscience. We come from God, who is the All, the perfect oneness...Life itself!

Now I will outline this journey from unity to separation and its return to unity. When we are born we are still very close to this Oneness. We enter the polar world; the world of separatism and as we advance in years we distance ourselves from our unitary origin, immersing ourselves in separatism. Could that be the reason why we believe that only children and the insane speak the truth? It may be that they are closer to the Oneness, they possess a more unitary natural wisdom, they more freely get in contact with the Collective Mind and they have been less contaminated by separatism, with its teachings and definitions loaded with artificial boundaries. Children have not yet entered it, and the insane refuse to live in 'The Empire of Prejudice' that is the world of 'normal people.'

We leave behind our first stage in the world of separatism at approximately six years of age. Perhaps that is why children younger than this age seem able to easily establish communication with animals, to learn any language and even to remember experiences that do not belong to any personal experience in their present life. They have the ability to enter inside the archives of the collective conscience or to remember passages of past lives.

Between the ages of six to twelve years old approximately, the child is trained in polar concepts. His/Her individualism is accentuated and he/she gradually loses the feeling of belonging to the whole; of

being a part of the cosmos, and of his/her sacred obligation to vibrate in harmony with all that surrounds us. The child is prepared to enter a stage of acute separatism and differentiation. During this stage it is often hard to tell a boy from a girl if they're dressed the same and wear the same hairstyle. Hair, skin, labial mucosa, bones and muscle system are all very similar in a boy and a girl.

Once puberty is reached the discharge of hormones from the sexual and reproductive glands leads us to fully enter the world of separatism. Now we come into full awareness of our nakedness, when exploiting the secondary sexual features of our bodies. Boys become angular, hairy, muscular, their voice acquires a deeper tone while girls become rounded, exuberant and more delicate than boys.

Little by little, this polarised world of contradictions and separatist feelings of exclusiveness becomes less threatening and more attractive for the adolescent. But regaining the lost paradise, the return to oneness, continues to be a dream caressed subconsciously. This is perhaps why we look for sex and mistake it for love, because in its climax for a fleeting moment we reach the ecstasy of the almost perfect oneness. Since this is a kind of oneness rarely promoted by love (on the contrary it is motivated by the quest for pleasure), it ends abruptly almost the very instant the orgasm reaches its end, leaving us empty.

This subconscious, yet intense, desire to find and experience oneness impels us to compulsively search for the constant repetition of the orgasmic experience.

In couples where orgasm takes place within the framework of a genuine loving relationship, the experience of oneness does not end abruptly when the orgasmic energy is extinguished. For this reason they are able to enjoy intimacy much more, with or without sex.

As we advance in age, first as adolescent, later as young adults and then as mature adults we forget our unitary origin. We unconditionally adhere to our separatism. We fall in love with polarity, our ego expands, and then almost without noticing it we are on our way back to oneness. We have entered the count down!

Our reproductive glands declare themselves on strike, the hormones for sexual differentiation go into decline, both in men and women, and once again we begin our sojourn towards what we call death, which is actually the birth into life within the oneness.

As we age, the differences between the sexes diminish. Even the differences in the hair colour disappears, the blond, the black, the native, sooner or later, on reaching their third age, adopt grey as their hair colour. Also, as we approach our journey's end, women's breasts and hips lose their roundness and muscles become atrophied in both sexes. If both sexes dress similarly and wear the same hairdo, it becomes almost impossible to tell them apart. As we return to the oneness consciousness becomes asexual.

Whether in an open or secretive way, sex, secondary sexual features, the well-defined and specific roles of each gender and polarity is of enormous importance to us. The onset of menstrual irregularities or of any other external manifestation reminds us that the period of marked differentiation is coming to an end, causing fear and resistance to the return trip. This, in turn, triggers the onset of the climacteric syndrome during menopause and a psychological and misguiding crisis in andropause (male menopause).

Premenstrual Syndrome

Here I refer to all the physical, mental and especially emotional changes that start taking place between two and fourteen days before menstruation. Changes that are alleviated almost immediately after the period of bleeding has begun. In the specific case of some women, the relevant feature of this syndrome is a change of mood towards a state of extreme irritability, expressed as irrational rage and sometimes accompanied by physical violence. Together with this external irritability comes the subjective feeling of tension. This is the reason why it is know as 'Premenstrual Tension Syndrome'.

The key trait of this syndrome is that symptoms disappear the very moment the bleeding begins and therefore it should not be confused with other complaints or discomfort due to the period itself. Some women suffer very painful periods even to the extent that, in some cases, they require pharmacological intervention and bed rest for a period of time. This is known as 'dysmenorrhoea' and is not what I am describing here. Contrary to what happens with the premenstrual syndrome, dysmenorrhoea settles on the first day of menstruation and goes away when menstruation ceases. It's usually characterised by spasmodic pain and a sensation of heaviness in the lower part of the abdomen, pelvis and back. There could be abdominal swelling and sometimes acute or alternating pain in the genital area.

Our mothers and grandmothers with their great empirical wisdom recommended those suffering from this problem to stay in bed with a hot water bottle placed on the lower part of the abdomen and/or lower back. Dysmenorrhoea responds well to a mixture of diuretic and analgesic medication, preferably a prostaglandin inhibitor. In many countries, health food stores sell natural diuretic drops or tablets. Our grandmothers used chamomile tea, which may be combined with one or two tablets of paracetamol every six or eight hours. Spasmodic Dysmenorrhoea is frequently attributed to the immaturity of the uterine muscles. The fact that it affects mostly young girls and women and tends to disappear with age and after the first pregnancies inclines me to believe that this theory has sufficient basis to be considered valid. Many women also report a certain degree of depression, headache and lack of physical, mental and sexual performance during their period. All of these symptoms are only maladies accompanying the period.

Premenstrual syndrome, as its name indicates is pre-period with the symptoms disappearing when it begins. The symptomatic orchestra of premenstrual syndrome include physical, mental and emotional symptoms that vary in number and intensity from one person to another. These symptoms include generalised swelling and weight gain due to fluid retention (a congestion and swelling of the abdomen, joints and fingers as well as congested and painful breasts). There may be a general sensation of being unwell, skin disorders, a change in eating habits and sleeping patterns.

Mental and emotional symptoms include a very wide range of manifestations, but probably the more disruptive are those affecting relationships. The sufferer starts presenting irrational emotional reactions out of proportion with the stimulus. These emotional outbursts become increasingly frequent. Anger runs out of control and paranoid reactions lead to physical violence, verbal abuse and apparently unmotivated crisis of tears and accusations.

As the trend of premenstrual syndrome is on the increase I wonder if in an age where women are waving flags against the patriarchal society, in which they have adopted and made their own many of the male's flaws; this syndrome is becoming more apparent, and therefore, better studied and reported. Our grandmothers were probably happier and more content with their natural attitudes, and thus suffered less from complaints arising from their most external and evident feminine features.

My intention is not to justify the fair or unfair distribution of roles the patriarchate assigns to each gender. I am merely pointing out that an envy of the masculine role and the total rejection of the perceived 'stereotyped concept' of femininity, which emotionally identifies the role assigned to women, is the cause of this syndrome and its associated problems. Perhaps this is why even the concept of beauty is changing, and for a long while the more glamourous models displayed very little external evidence of their femineity and beauty as they become more and more unisex. These models presented themselves as flat; the antithesis of Venus or Eve. This standard of beauty imposed by the emperors of fashion, many of whom appear to be markedly confused over their own sexual identity, may reflect an envy of those exquisitely feminine forms to which they will never be able to aspire. I hope that this trend will disappear.

Those emotionally well-balanced are learning to relate to the opposite sex in a more friendly way. Within a social framework of camaraderie they share sport, academic and cultural activities. They accept the opposite sex without reserve and appreciate their own image and the external manifestations of their own sexuality. They are also inadvertently bringing into the world of fashion a whole new trend of a more dynamic, natural and healthy looking model, which in my opinion that is genuinely more beautiful even if less glamourous.

There are a large number of books and articles that describe in detail the physical violence that takes place in the homes of sufferers of premenstrual syndrome. I write sufferers in plural because the woman's partner and children suffer the scaring consequences of the verbal and physical abuse frequently occurring in the home. A peaceful, harmonious life is difficult to achieve when living with someone who suffers from premenstrual syndrome. The tendency to hit her children or throw objects can cause a lot of harm and is retrospectively tragic for a mother.

I wonder if the mental and emotional components of this syndrome are only the consequence of some bio-chemical imbalance or if the bio-chemical imbalance is the consequence of a thinking and emotional pattern in which the woman who suffers from PMS is the victim of her own gender envy? Could this be the explanation of the successful outcome achieved when using testosterone as a treatment of the symptoms?

Could it be that the intensity with which a woman desires and envies the masculine role within family, society and the heterosexual relationship framework provoke in her a strong rejection of her own femineity? A lacerating frustration and an insatiable resentment towards men in general and especially the one who is her partner? Is her partner the lightning rod where she deposits the reasoning of her unconfessed hatred? Could it be that if he possesses admirable traits it gives her more reason to hate him since he represents the man she wishes to be?

It is my belief that a perfect understanding and joyful acceptance of the fact that both genders are poles of the one and same reality, that we are complementary and healthily interdependent, that the role each plays within an affective and sexual relationship are the result of a free agreement inspired in love. Then cooperation and mutual affinity of resonance is the path that will progressively lead to transcend the premenstrual syndrome.

VIOLENCE

'Where the streets are beautiful and smooth but
the people prefer the side roads. Where the rules of
court are strict but the fields are full of weeds.
Where the barns are quiet empty but garments are
beautiful and glamourous. Where every one girds
himself with a sharp word. Where eating and
drinking habits are refined and goods are
abundant. There rules confusion, not government.'
Lao Tze The Tao Teh Ching

Violence is a term almost impossible to define in the abstract. We come to understand it's meaning by experiencing, feeling, repressing, exercising or from suffering it. Is it an attitude adopted with the purpose of intimidating? Is it a behaviour? Is it an emotion? Is it part of our survival instinct? Is it a little bit of all of them? Or is it a way of thinking originated from a particular perception system?

Sourcing literature on this phenomenon doesn't help since philosophers, thinkers and educators either haven't bothered or haven't been able to define it. In order to describe violence we must showcase the facts, their consequences, the circumstances surrounding it and the possible explanation of its cause. Even following this process the questions of the previous paragraph are not easily answered.

On television, radio or in the newspapers we are confronted daily with military, political, economic, social and religious violence—all different modalities of terrorism. We are confronted with the violence of common criminals, murderers, attackers, rapists, burglars and white collar offenders; with road violence (a very generalised form of terrorism), traffic accidents and of those who speed and drive their cars in a manner which is imprudent and criminal; with the violence of those who run over a woman, a child, an old person or a dog and then fleeing the scene of the accident leaving behind a trail of grief and death; with the violence of vandals who destroy or deface public and private property; with domestic violence of abusive husbands, wives, parents, children or siblings; with the violence of youth gangs, drug's traffickers and protection extortionists; with the violence imposed on us by suicidal individuals who, actually or imaginary, feel themselves to have been the victims of violence; with the violence of rightist or leftist military dictatorships; with the violence of fascist, communist and socialist; with the violence of pacifist, machoists (male chauvinists), feminists, gays and lesbians; with the violence of the cynics who scorn any feelings of tenderness—and on and on it goes.

Each act of violence is placed in a different label by the media. We read and hear about 'social', 'revolutionary', 'domestic', 'racial', 'ethnic', 'sport' violence all which continues until we reach the most adequate of labels: irrational. There is only one type of violence that simultaneously manifests at an infinite variety of levels...the irrational!

Violence is based on the ego, and this is an irrationality that all beings of earth, not only human, share. The arrogance of any ego is the key trait which leads us to believe that we are the only beings on the planet to have one. Our ego, as the con artist it is, has tricked us into believing that its existence is based on our thinking and imagination. This blinds us to the fact that it is founded, originated and nourished by fear. Fear such as fear of living; of dying; of failure or success; of intimacy; of rejection; of inadequate education; of weakness; of power; of what others say or think and fear of the unknown. This includes the fear of being presented with proof that we are not as superior as we would like to think we are. That feeling of superiority which gave foundation to racism, elitism, classism, nationalism and western official political terrorism as opposed to the middle east and revolutionary terrorism.

There is also fear of being wrong (regarding religion, politics, sport etc); fear of desertion or loneliness (dependency, addiction, co-dependency); fear of the opposite gender; fear of our own sexuality; social fear, including apprehension about our projected image, and so the list grows.

Depending on a few other personality traits, and in accordance with them, our ego will dress-up each type of fear in a specific disguise. These fears will frequently, and under camouflage, endeavour to appear as exactly the opposite. If we feel assaulted by our own 'inner fear', one usually unknown even to ourselves, we will strive to project this aggression outwards in order to feel better. This external projection is what we call violence. As violence intimidates and terrifies it generates a chain reaction of more fear and more violence. So to attempt to eliminate terrorism by imposing fear produces exactly the opposite effect.

As we can easily deduce, violence is nothing but a consequence of an internal 'fear', sometimes hidden at the very core of our existence, or in the nucleus of each and every one of our body's cells. Is it our original sin? Is it still waiting for redemption?

Each of the 'illuminated' who have visited this planet, brought us messages of love and forgiveness, peace and co-operation—have indicated to us the path to follow. One of them, Jesus of Nazareth said: 'I am the way, the truth and the life, only through me may you reach the Father'. Only through love may we reach the Father. For love is the vessel which transcends fear, and therefore violence...and therefore terrorism. Love transcends ego, and without ego there is no jealousy, no eagerness to possess, no competitiveness.

J. Krishnamurti, when speaking about violence stated:

> 'We must look into this phenomenon of violence by first observing the violence within ourselves and then the external kind. It may be that once we have understood the violence within ourselves we need not observe the external kind any more, *since what we project outwards is only what we are inside.* The fact is we are violent humans. There are thousands of explanations for this violence. If we become engrossed in them we may lose our way because experts tell us this is the cause of violence. The more explanations we come by, the more certain we are to have understood what violence is; but things remain the same. Please keep in mind that a description is

not the same as what is being explained. There are many explanations that are reasonably simple and obvious—crowded cities, excess population, inheritance and all else related. We can leave all that aside. The fact remains...we are violent people. From childhood we are brought up to be violent, competitive, and brutal with one another. We are the conflict, and we live with this conflict. We are always in conflict, in constant struggle and in contradiction, at home, in the office and even while we sleep.'

Marxist, communist, socialist and leftist of all styles and types, believe they have seen in the injustice of the capitalist society, the roots that nourish human violence. But for seventy-three years they ruled half of the planet and violence didn't disappear from the places in which they attempted to implement their perfect society. The Bolshevik Revolution, under the excuse of establishing a solid base for a vigorous development of socialism, 'brought to justice' millions of Russian citizens accused of co-operating with the Czars and of exploiting bourgeois, counter-revolutionaries and so on.

Joseph Stalin, in a wealth of cruelty, continued this bloodbath of persecution and execution of eighteen million Russians! Not even Hitler committed genocide to such a scale. The horrors of Mao Tse Tung, Pol Pot and Fidel Castro wane the atrocities of Idi Amin or Saddam Hussein. The purges and inclement persecution of dissidents within the communist systems meet their equal in the unending and harrowing 'Holy Wars' of Islamic fanatics, the 'Crusades' of fundamentalist Christians and the horrors committed by the Inquisition.

The erection of walls, such as in Berlin, to separate the 'Newly Born and Pure Socialist Society' from the 'contaminated and corrupted capitalist society' was done at a high cost. A cost in lives, jailings, trials, as well as in a high dose of frustration, grief and tears from a people forced to erect stupid artificial borders of separatism while deep in their hearts their common ethnic, linguistic, human and historical roots kept alive their longing for unity.

Feminists insist on blaming the structures and attitudes of the patriarchate for all the injustices and cases of 'reactive violence' (to give a label denoting a violent reaction to an also violent cause). However, the growth and widespread development of the feminist movement has not brought about a decrease in violence, on the contrary, domestic violence has peaked in countries where feminism has experienced growth. Women who twenty or thirty years ago had few traffic accidents are now keeping up statistically with the men.

Tobaccoism, alcoholism and drug addiction, all which result from problems of communication, are also increasing at an alarming rate amongst women. Also, the number of women killing their offspring dramatically increased as women adopted attitudes that were conventionally masculine. The higher incidence of cholesterol, arterial hypertension, heart attacks, cerebral-vascular accidents and premenstrual Syndrome within the female population is parallel to the change in attitudes promoted by feminists.

Some sociologists believe that sexual information, and sexual education, easy access to contraceptives and needle interchange programs eventually will suppress the wave of rapes, abortions and sexually transmitted diseases. Never before in the history of this planet has the human race enjoyed so much sexual information, access to condoms, needles and clinics specialising in contraception and abortion. Yet the murder and violence towards helpless human beings whom we call by the technical name of 'foetus' has not diminished, on the contrary, it has increasingly become one of the favourite ways of contraception. Sexually transmitted diseases have not disappeared and AIDS has reached epidemic proportions! Also violent rape and sexual abuse are occurring daily.

Psychologists and marriage counsellors proliferated in the second half of the twentieth century and still do in developed countries. Responsibility for the behaviour and conduct of the young and adolescents was blamed on parental and family errors, childhood trauma or abuse (psychological model) or on the unfair social structures (social model). School and workplace counsellors invaded society, did this cause juvenile delinquency to decrease or vandalism to disappear? Did it lower the divorce rate? Did the number of violent acts diminish?

Pseudo-scientists have been talking about different techniques of gene modification. Genes have been blamed for diabetes, obesity, heart disease, multiple sclerosis, mental illness, cancer, osteo-arthritis and many other diseases and disorders including violence and addictive personality. After decades of abuse of genetic modification violence and addictive personalities are still increasing. The medical model with their quick fix is a joke!

For a long time man has been searching for the external causes of violence and once he believes he has found them he will wage battle in order to gain control of them. 'However, the irrefutable fact is that man is still the same as he has been for millions of years; quarrelsome, covetous, jealous, violent and overwhelmed by great suffering.' —J. Krishnamurti.

In a commendable effort to search within each individual for the causes of violence, man set out to study physiological traits trying to establish a link between the external facial and physical features with the internal tendencies and structures of the consciousness. Research on the type of head shape, forehead inclination, degree of nasal protuberance and eye separation, facial angle, labial rictus when smiling, height at which ears were positioned on the skull etc proliferated. This science was called 'phrenology'. Unfortunately the strong racist tendencies of the time used this science to spread totally unfounded theories of racial superiority. Was man beginning to understand that thoughts and emotions could mould and determine physical features? Some day humanity will take up this research again, probably giving to it another name. Perhaps next time mankind does this research, if free of racial prejudice, the results will be more thorough and successful.

Some astrologers would have us to believe that the degree of violence in a person stems from the position of Mars on his/her birth chart. A very nice attempt of eluding blame, placing the responsibility on a celestial body light years away!

The position of the planet Mars in any birth chart is only indicative of the degree of spiritual evolution that a particular individual piece of consciousness has in regard to violence at the moment of birth. An astrological chart is only a faithful and accurate representation, at an outerspace level, of the characteristics of the person to whom it belongs just as the genetic map is at a biological-chromosomal level.

Neither the astrological chart, nor the genetic map is the cause of violence. They are only simultaneous manifestations of the same reality at different levels. Nevertheless, this reality is previous to the astrological or genetic maps and determines the structure of the latter. In no way do the structures of these maps determine the manifestations of the consciousness.

The Tao is represented as a circle made up of two halves, the 'Yang' (the masculine, creative, active) and the 'Yin' (the feminine, receptive, passive). The combination and sum of both these two halves results in a whole, beautiful, strong, intelligent and functional individual since each half, on its own, is incomplete and lacks real existence. The sky wouldn't be bright nocturnally if galaxies, solar systems and stars did not exist and stars would have nowhere to be if there were no skies. The earth would perish, disintegrate and disappear without plants and animals, and animals and plants need the planet to exist. The poles do not exclude each other, they are opposites but not antagonistic. Each depends upon the other for its existence and future development. Balance is salvation and integration. When balance is cultivated during our life-span the result is peaceful longevity.

Some new age feminists justify the increasing violence in modern women by saying that in the process of integration of opposites at an individual level, many women 'integrate their inner male'. An inner male who is chauvinist, violent, rude and inconsiderate as well as promiscuous. This is yet another wonderfully homophobic way of escaping from responsibility by placing it on the anonymous being of the male gender. For affinity of resonance, the inner male or female inside each of us is but the identical twin of the male or female living and fulfilling his/her role on the outside.

There is no escape of social, racial, domestic, sexual, economic, political or religious violence or terrorism. Since it is the result of a system of perception based on fear, not love. This defective perception system will not be overcome through struggle or war, but will be transcended by co-operation and service.

Struggle may see an escalation in the achievement of just vindications but never will it diminish, in any way, the phenomenon of violence. We will witness an age where refuges will be established to protect abused same sex partners, this will happen because the sexist explanation of the phenomenon of violence is passionately simplistic.

Violence generates violence, struggle generates struggle, and terrorism will not be transcended by any war but only through understanding, acceptance, love and balance. Action does not mean struggle. Activists like Martin Luther King Jr. or Mahatma Gandhi were true examples of non-violence, but they were 'Holistic activists'. They declared themselves in favour of human rights and showed a spiritual standing heavy with love and understanding.

After thousands of years of evolution and technological development tribal man came down from caves dug deep in high mountain walls, covered their nakedness with clothes, protected his feet with footwear and disguised their threatening grin by lifting their lips and baring their teeth under the mask of a smile. He also learnt to hide his claws and decided to live in the dense forests of large cities.

We are now at the dawn of the twenty-first century of the Christian era and within our reach are telephones, mobile phones, fax machines, computerised images, ultrasonic transport, micro-waves, nuclear radiation treatments supposedly to cure some diseases, drugs capable of mimicking the natural neuro-transmitters of our bodies, accurate methods of forecasting meteorological change, alarms and counteralarm systems, radars and cameras operated from satellites, all this and much more, yet man is still the same violent, quarrelsome, competitive, brutal, cruel, destructive caveman of prehistoric times.

There is an evident disproportion; a disharmony between evolution and technological development; between physical, technological development and the progress of our consciousness. A disharmony artificially provoked and socially constructed by the materialistic tendencies of science and the almost exclusively external motivation of our investigative processes, which have brought about an erroneous and simultaneous display of solutions.

There is within humans an insatiable thirst for 'The Meaning of Life'. We instinctively know that life has a purpose, a meaning that transcends our individuality. The creationist and evolutionist theories about the universe are not antagonistic, nor do they exclude each other. The 'Divine Power of Life' and its direct intervention in universal events does not necessarily come into question if we believe in evolution. The belief in evolutionary processes need not ignore the relevance and the directive power of the spirit over matter, otherwise it would force us to only partially explain our sensitivity towards beauty, art, desires, resentment and most of all unconditional love, abnegation and heroism. Do not the laws that rule evolution and the changes in DNA speak of the existence of a Great Legislator?

To the scientific world evolution is a genetic process of learning, where organisms are refined and improved through the genes of the survivors (survival of the fittest). To assume evolution has no purpose is to place the human mind way over the cosmic mind. We can search within ourselves for the meaning of life and the purpose of evolution, or we can avoid the responsibility of the quest and take refuge in the materialistic, technical and simplistic explanations of science.

Science has become another weapon of dominion and control of a domineering culture and domineering social classes. The working class, unemployed and common professionals have no access of entry into the fields of very expensive laboratories. Science methodology is only another way of maintaining class division. In this way the owners of 'big capital' belong not only to the aristocracy of financial, political and military power but also to the aristocracy of intelligence. They were self-erected as the maximum authority which determines truth; what is valid and what is crap. In this way any evidence that goes against the system is branded as not valid.

We know that when treating neurosis, any traumatic experience needs to be consciously acknowledged before it can be overcome and transcended. If, for whatever reason, we avoid acknowledging the traumatic experience at a conscious level and opt to sweep it under the carpet, it will fight relentlessly to be acknowledged, accepted and transcended, forcing us to go through the experience as many times as necessary until it is acknowledged. This, obviously, generates discomfort, frustration, escapism, struggle and resistance. In a word...violence!

At the genesis of any neurosis there is a subconscious feeling of guilt from which we are trying to escape. This feeling of guilt makes us go through the traumatic experience again and again, so that we learn to face it, redeem it and transcend it.

Has the human mind, as the collective mind of our species, a congenital and hidden sense of guilt? Is this the 'original sin'? Is the redemption and transcending of this original sin the meaning of life? Does this redemption embrace a journey of self-discovery? Is the transcendence of violence linked to the redemption of this sense of guilt? Is it possible to transcend this guilty feeling without embarking in our self-discovery journey?

Identifying and accepting this congenital guilt will help us perceive the meaning of life. If you perceive your meaning, you perceive your destiny. To think that we exist only as the offspring of a shapeless mass of carbonic gas mixed with hydrogen, to which an accidental electrical or magnetic charge provided the necessary information to agglutinate and become a living cell, and that our destiny is to compete for the acquisition of consumer goods, doesn't help us to transcend violence, and only benefits the manufacturers of the consumerist society.

When we distance ourselves from genuine spirituality (not religious Puritanism) the manifestations of violence increase despite improvements in the economical, social, cultural, technological, sporting or academic environments. Violence does not disappear with the working class conquering their vindications, or with women obtaining the right to vote, or with gays and lesbians being able to raise the banner on their sexual preferences, nor by the access to education for all. Neither will it disappear by jailing and executing every delinquent, or by preforming a frontal lobotomy and/or sterilisation on those evidently violent.

Neither will it disappear by manufacturing drugs for happiness, for relaxation (tranquillisers and anxiety regulators), painkillers or serotonin uptake stimulant or inhibitors. Nor by neutralising the neuro-transmitters that stimulate aggressive impulses, nor by eliminating the gene responsible for violence.

Violence will disappear when the human race reaches sufficient spiritual maturity to voluntarily and consciously acknowledge and accept its sense of mission. A mission that targets the crowning of love as the supreme sovereign of the universe. Then mankind will be able to live according to this purpose, and therefore, to its destiny.

Obviously we are walking away from this objective. As long as we are escaping from the real meaning of life, as long as science is leading us away from the spiritual world our societies increase their rate of violence. Inside industrialised societies even music and other expressions of art are becoming increasingly violent.

Art that expresses love, or tenderness, have less market acceptance than art that expresses frustration, rage, hate, resentment and revenge. Rap and heavy rock music are widely accepted because it is becoming increasingly difficult to identify ourselves with expressions of love and tenderness. The feelings of rage, frustration and revenge of heavy rock and rap singers are easily shared by a significant number of society members as they hold similar feelings.

Industrialised societies are providing people with more commodities and facilities but not with peace of mind or with happiness. Frustration and rage increases at a similar rate to societies irrational buyer/consumer expectations of what sells and what doesn't. When the government of the 'most civilised nation of this planet' talks about the killing of thirty-two thousand civilians, branding it 'collateral damages,' then something is seriously wrong.

When we cease to praise those who avoid internal dialogue; when we cease to emulate those who display power without consideration of the suffering engendered; when we reject those who consider the killing of thousands of civilians as 'collateral damage'; when we no longer label as 'weird' or 'crazy' those who search for the hidden purpose of life; when we start to appreciate the poet more and to envy the magnate less; when we are able to love all life on the earth and in the oceans; when we come to understand that the lost paradise is to be found in the oneness within diversity, then and only then, will we be on the path to transcend violence and disease. Violence as a disorder or disease is an external manifestation of some particular individuals or social state of consciousness.

> 'Blessed are the pure of heart, they will be called the children of God.'

> 'True words are not beautiful, beautiful words are not true. Competence does not persuade, persuasion is not competent. The sage is not learned; the learned man is not wise. The man of calling does not heap up possessions. The more he does for others, the more he possesses. The more he gives to others, the more he has. The Tao of

heaven is furthering without causing harm. The
Tao of the man of calling is to be effective without
quarrelling.'

Lao Tze *The Tao Teh Ching*